Kruschevlje

This book is dedicated to my children

Kruschevlje

Concentration Camp for German-Yugoslavs after World War II

Therese Herscha (Schmidt) and
Ricardo Quiñónez
Proofread by: Janice Quiñónez Cabral

2007

*Cover image: Amalia Quiring (Herscha),
with sons Nikolaus and Adam*

Kruschevlje

Katharina Gyori (Frey) and Maria Frey (Herscha)

*In memory of my grandmother Katharina who lost
her life in a concentration camp, and my parents
Adam and Maria Herscha for all of their suffering
throughout the war and captivity in Kruschevlje*

TABLE OF CONTENTS

ACKNOWLEDGEMENTS

To Sydney Schmidt, for the many hours she spent gathering and preparing the family photographs that were included in my book.

To Ricardo Quiñónez, who encouraged me to write this book. I am grateful that he helped me put in writing all of the memories that came back to me from years ago. Thank you so much!

To Janice, for not giving up until the completion of my book, working hard correcting our mistakes over and over again and helping us until it was finished.

To my friends Jakob Lessmeister and Gerdi Herzog, who were so helpful while I was putting my book together.

First Generation

I.Nikolaus Herscha I was born around 1848 in Karlsdorf, Banat, Yugoslavia.

Nikolaus I married Magdalena Bogdan who was born around 1855 and died around 1935.

They had the following children:

+ 2 M i. Nikolaus Herscha II, who was born around 1878.

+ 3 F ii. Katharina Herscha, who married Mr. Saharias.

SECOND GENERATION

2. Nikolaus Herscha II (Nikolaus I) was born around 1878 in Karlsdorf, Banat, Yugoslavia and died at the end of WWI.

Nikolaus II married Amalia Quiring in 1907. She was born Roman Catholic on March 10, 1882 in Karlsdorf, Banat, Yugoslavia. She died when she was struck by lightning around 1916 in her hometown.

Nikolaus II and Amalia had the following children:

+ 4 M i. Nikolaus Herscha III, born in 1908 in Karlsdorf, Banat, Yugoslavia.
+ 5 M ii. Adam Herscha, born on June 18, 1911 in Karlsdorf, Banat, Yugoslavia and died on March 24, 1985.

THIRD GENERATION

4. Nikolaus Herscha III (Nikolaus II, Nikolaus I) was born in 1908 in Karlsdorf, Banat, Yugoslavia. He was captured during WWII, after that he was reunited with his family in Germany, where he died around 1952.

Nikolaus III married Barbara Mulitsch, they had the following children:

+   6   M   i.   Josef Herscha, born in 1930 in Karlsdorf, Banat, Yugoslavia.
+   7   M   ii.   Nikolaus Herscha IV, born in 1936 in Karlsdorf, Banat, Yugoslavia.

5. Adam Herscha (Nikolaus II, Nikolaus I) was born on June 18, 1911 in Karlsdorf, Banat, Yugoslavia and died on March 24, 1985 in Chicago, Illinois U.S.A.

Adam married Maria Frey, daughter of Ernst Frey and Katharina Gyori, on November 25, 1931 in Gross Betschkerek (now known as Zrenjanin), Banat, Yugoslavia. Maria Frey was born on October 24, 1912 in Gross Betschkerek, Banat, Yugoslavia and died on February 22, 2003 in Palos Hills, Illinois, U.S.A.

They had the following children:

+ 8 F i. Therese Herscha, born in Gross Betschkerek, Banat, Yugoslavia.

+ 9 F ii. _____ Herscha, born in Gross Betschkerek, Banat, Yugoslavia.

+ 10 F iii. G e r t r u d e Herscha, born in Gross Betschkerek, Banat, Yugoslavia.

Maria and Adam Herscha

Maria Frey, Katharina Gyori (Frey) and husband Ernst Frey

German-Yugoslavian Soldier Ernst Frey, Jr.

Left to right: Therese Gyori (Kodel), Mrs. Gyori, Katharina Gyori (Frey) and Mrs. Frey; standing in front: Therese Herscha

FOURTH GENERATION

6. Josef Herscha (Nikolaus III, Nikolaus II, Nikolaus I) was born in 1930 in Karlsdorf, Banat, Yugoslavia.

Josef married Maria Watza. They had the following Children:

+ II F i. Irmgard Herscha, born in 1954 in Germany, Europe.
+ 12 M ii. Josef Herscha, born in Germany, Europe.
+ 13 M iii. Theodor Herscha, born in 1958 in Chicago, Illinois U.S.A.

7. Nikolaus Herscha IV (Nikolaus III, Nikolaus II, Nikolaus I) was born in Karlsdorf, Banat, Yugoslavia.

Nikolaus IV married Rosalia Kolb and they had the following children:

+ 14 M i. Nikolaus Herscha V, born in 1959 in Chicago, Illinois, U.S.A.
+ 15 f ii. Ramona Herscha, born in 1964 in Chicago, Illinois U.S.A.

8. Therese Herscha (Adam, Nikolaus II, Nikolaus I) was born in Gross Betschkerek, Banat, Yugoslavia.

Therese married Stefan Schmidt in 1950 in Lager Haid, Linz, Austria, son of Andreas Schmidt and Rosalia Gross. Stefan was born on July 6, 1929 in Vukovar, Croatia, Yugoslavia. He died on March 5, 1996 in Chicago, Illinois, U.S.A.

They had one child:

    +   16   M   i.   S t e f a n Schmidt, born on May 5, 1951.

9. _____ Herscha (Adam, Nikolaus II, Nikolaus I).
    Married Mr._____.

They had the following children:

    +   17   F   i.   _____.
    +   18   M   ii.   _____.
    +   19   F   iii.   _____.

10 .Gertrude Herscha (Adam, Nikolaus II, Nikolaus I) was born in Gross Betschkerek, Banat, Yugoslavia.

Gertrude married Wolfgang Buhler on August 21, 1964 in Chicago, Illinois, U.S.A. Wolfgang was born on February 8, 1942.

They had the following children:

    +   20   F   i.   Heidi Buhler, born in 1965, Chicago, Illinois, U.S.A.

+ 21 M ii. Robert Buhler, born on January 16, 1969 in Chicago, Illinois, U.S.A.

+ 22 F iii. Monika Buhler, born on April 17, 1973 in Chicago, Illinois, U.S.A.

The Herscha Family, 1942

FIFTH GENERATION

11. Irmgard Herscha (Josef, Nikolaus III, Nikolaus II, Nikolaus I) was born in 1954 in Germany, Europe.

Irmgard married Bill Jauch. They had the following children:

      23   F   i.   Tanya Jauch, born in Norridge, Illinois, U.S.A.
      24   F   ii.   Sandra Jauch, born in Norridge, Illinois, U.S.A.

12. Josef Herscha (Nikolaus III, Nikolaus II, Nikolaus I).

Josef married Judy Orrel. They had the following children:

      25   M   i.   Cody Herscha.

14. Nikolaus Herscha V (Nikolaus IV, Nikolaus III, Nikolaus II, Nikolaus I) was born in 1959 in Chicago, Illinois, U.S.A.

Nikolaus V married Linda Binger and they had the following children:

      26   F   i.   Britaney Herscha.

15. Ramona Herscha (Nikolaus IV, Nikolaus III, Nikolaus II, Nikolaus I) was born in 1964 in Chicago, Illinois, U.S.A.

Ramona had the following children:

27	F	i.	Nicole.
28	F	ii.	Melisa.

16. Stefan Schmidt (Therese Herscha, Adam, Nikolaus II, Nikolaus I) was born on May 5, 1951 in Lager Haid, Ober Österreich (Upper Austria), Europe.

Stefan married Sydney Klein in St. Benedict Church on June 10, 1971 in Chicago, Illinois, U.S.A. They had the following children:

+ 29 M i. Steven C. Schmidt, born on September 28, 1974.
+ 30 M ii. Michael S. Schmidt, born on February 9, 1978.

17._____ (_____ Herscha, Adam, Nikolaus II, Nikolaus I)
_____ married _____.

They had one child:

31 F i. _____.

19._____ (_____ Herscha, Adam, Nikolaus II, Nikolaus I).

She married _____ and they had the following children:

32	F	i.	_____.
33	M	ii.	_____.

20. Heidi Buhler (Gertrude Herscha, Adam, Nikolaus II, Nikolaus I) was born in 1965 in Chicago, Illinois, U.S.A.

Heidi married Pierre Archambeault. Pierre was born in 1958. They had the following children:

       34   M   i. Joseph Archambeault, born on December 30, 1987 in Chicago, Illinois, U.S.A.
       35   F   ii.   Nicole Archambeault, born on August 20, 1990 in Chicago, Illinois, U.S.A.

21. Robert Buhler (Gertrude Herscha, Adam, Nikolaus II, Nikolaus I) was born on January 16, 1969 in Chicago, Illinois, U.S.A.

Robert married Shirley Young in the city of Chicago, Illinois. They had the following children:

       36   F   i.   Tatiana Buhler, born on January 25, 1991 in Chicago, Illinois, U.S.A.
       37   F   ii.   Gabriela Buhler, born in 1995 in Chicago, Illinois, U.S.A.

22. Monika Buhler (Gertrude Herscha, Adam, Nikolaus II, Nikolaus I) was born on April 17, 1973 in Chicago, Illinois, U.S.A.

Monika and Joe Vale had one child:

38 F i. Daniella Gertrude Vale was born on March 6, 2006 in Wisconsin, U.S.A.

Stefan Schmidt, Jr.
When he graduated from High School

SIXTH GENERATION

29. Steven C. Schmidt (Stefan Schmidt, Therese Herscha, Adam, Nikolaus II, Nikolaus I) was born on September 28, 1974 in Maywood, Illinois, U.S.A.

Steven married Joy Mikulic, daughter of Jim Mikulic and Ida Carswell, in 1999 in Marine Valley Community Church, Palos Hills, Illinois. Joy was born August 6, 1977 in Oak Lawn, Illinois, U.S.A.

They had the following children:

     39   F   i.   Shayna Rose Schmidt, born on April 13, 2000 in Palos Hills, Illinois, U.S.A.
     40   F   ii.   Haley Caroline Schmidt, born on June 29, 2002 in the city of Palos Hills, Illinois, U.S.A.
     41   F   iii.   Zoey Therese Schmidt, born on October 13, 2005 in Palos Hills, Illinois, U.S.A.

30. Michael S. Schmidt (Stefan Schmidt, Therese Herscha, Adam, Nikolaus II, Nikolaus I) was born on February 9, 1978 in Maywood, Illinois, U.S.A.

Michael married Toni Matkovich, daughter of Paul Matkovich and Alix Schafer, on July 7, 2000 in Garden Wedding Chapel, Bridgeview, Illinois. Toni was born on January 1, 1980 in Chicago Illinois, U.S.A.

Michael and Toni had the following children:

        42   F   i.   AbigailCindySchmidt, born on October 24, 2000 in Berwyn Illinois, U.S.A.

        43   F   ii.   Addison   Rose Schmidt, born on October 12, 2004 in Oak Lawn, Illinois U.S.A.

GROSS BETSCHKEREK, 1941

I will never forget the uproar of the German-Yugoslavian people when Adolf Hitler ordered his German army to invade Yugoslavia in 1941 during World War II. Every German descendant living in Gross Betschkerek, now known as Zrenjanin, went out to Haupt Gasse, the main street, to greet the soldiers. At least 10,000 German descendants were living in the city at the time. Flags were displayed from each German-Yugoslavian house, including ours. Our next-door neighbor displayed his Hungarian flag instead, opposing the newcomers. It was an all day parade and full of excitement. My friends were walking all over the city with their parents waving small German flags.

As a child, I remember Gross Betschkerek being a nice city to live in. My father and his Jewish business partner owned a fur factory where they worked all day long. My mother was home taking care of my little sister Kathy and me. Every year a farmer came to our house in his wagon to deliver bacon, schinken, ham, bratwurst, headcheese, etc. and to fill our wooden containers with farina, sugar and flour. The farmer used rope to hang each of the meats from hooks on the ceiling of our attic. He would also hang grapes from long strings which I used to like to jump and get. Those grapes were delicious! He would bring enough of a supply so that it would last us throughout the winter. We had a maid who would come to our house to cook and clean and do the laundry. She would broil duck and goose and preserve them by dipping them in their own fat and keeping them in special containers in the attic to eat during the winter.

At the factory, my father paid a man to run errands and make deliveries for him. The man had a horse carriage and during the school year there were times when my father would send him to drive me to or from school. I didn't like riding in the carriage. I had more fun when I walked with the other kids in my neighborhood. I remember one day my mother called me to try on a fur coat and hat that my father had made for me for the coming winter. I liked the fur hat but since the other kids didn't have one they used to tease me about it. On the mornings when the driver picked me up from my house, as soon as he turned the corner I always took the hat off and put it under my arm. Before I returned home I would make sure to put it on so my mother wouldn't know I wasn't wearing it.

Shortly after the invasion, my father was called to join the German Army so he had to go to war as a paramedic. While he was away, he left his business partner looking after their fur factory. It was about two years later that Yugoslav-Partisans took over Gross Betschkerek. German soldiers asked all German descendants or any person whose last name was of German origin, to evacuate the city. There was a population of about twenty-five to thirty thousand people made up of Bulgarians, Serbians, Hungarians, Jews and others who could stay because they were not in danger like we were.

Left to right: Therese Herscha, Katharina Gyori (Frey), Maria Frey (Herscha), walking in Gross Betschkerek, 1939

Soldiers knocked from door to door ordering all German-Yugoslavians to go to the train station and not to worry because we would be back in a matter of weeks. My youngest sister Gertrude was only a baby at the time. She was born after my father had come home on a short leave from the war. After my father had left, my mother wrote him a letter letting him know that he was going to be a father again. He wrote back saying "if it is a boy, you know what you are going to name him and if it is a girl you can choose her name," so she chose the name Gertrude. Since my mother was home alone with us, and without a male figure in the house, she did not know whether to leave or stay. Doctor Janko, who belonged to the Cultur-Bund, talked to my mother and advised her, as a friend of the family, to leave the city as soldiers were ordering. My grandfather, Ernst Frey, also told my mother to leave for a while and urged my grandmother, Katharina Frey, to go with us. Reluctantly, my mother decided to do as her father was urging. My grandfather decided he would stay taking care of the house and working at his small business until we came back home. He probably thought we would return in a few weeks, as they told us. Little did we know that we wouldn't return until 1987.

The next day my mother, Maria Frey Herscha, my grandmother, my sisters Kathy and Gertrude, and I, Therese Herscha, made our way to the train station. As soon as we got there, we were loaded onto a cargo train without the slightest idea of where we were being taken at that moment. The train wasn't very long with only about three cars. I can't guess how many people were shoved into each car. Those who owned horses or wagons were asked to go on their own towards Nieder, Austria (Lower Austria) or Germany until things settled down. We sat on the wooden floor not being able to move freely but we could at least stretch our legs some or stand up here and there. The teenagers made sure that the elderly and children were as comfortable as possible. The evacuation lasted about a week. Train after train left Gross Betschkerek, loaded with families and soldiers to Austria. A man was assigned to be the leader in each car to direct people and tell them what to do. My mother and grandmother brought along plenty of luggage and two containers with goose and duck to eat during the trip. They had also brought money in case of any emergencies.

Some people refused to leave Gross Betschkerek because they had too much to lose—farms, houses, farm animals, money, land. They didn't want to leave everything they owned behind. They were stubborn and stayed. Maybe they thought the Serbian Communists wouldn't bother them since they had never displayed a picture of Hitler in their homes, the Hakenkreuz flag (swastika), never went to any political meetings, didn't belong to any political party, let alone wear the swastika emblem pin fastened on their collars. They were wrong! All Yugoslav-Partisans at Gross Betschkerek knew who they were, so they were captured by the Partisan Guerrilla and sent into concentration camps like Rudolfsgnad, Sekitsch, Kruschevlje, Jarek, Gakovo and many others I cannot remember. After the war was over I heard that some of them were sold as slaves to rich communists or military people, to work in farms that were taken away from German-Yugoslavians by the Partisan Communist Party. Properties were taken away from hard working German-Yugoslavian families who had inherited the land from their ancestors and were given to big shots as well as to poor members of the Serbian Party for cheap rent. They wanted all German-Yugoslavian people out of Yugoslavia or dead! I heard in those days that the big shots who belonged to the Nazi Party, fled from the city long before the German army started to evacuate all German descendents out of Yugoslavia. I wonder if they came back home after the war ended, and I hope they had also run the same luck we had.

A few hours after our train had left Gross Betschkerek, we stopped in a deserted area and were told to get off the train. After about fifteen minutes they told us that we would stay there for at least two hours, so my grandmother got a fire going and my mother warmed up some goose. To us children it was like going on a picnic. The trip lasted about four days, stopping several times during the day to eat or take care of any other necessities. One time they told us that we would be at the rest stop for about one to two hours. People got off the train and went to stretch their legs and look for a nice place to eat lunch or lay on the wild grass not realizing how far away from the train they were getting. After a short time the train whistle went off and the train started to move forward. Our leader started yelling at us to get aboard in a hurry. Everybody started to run after the moving train, afraid of being left there, leaving many goods and food behind in the process. After that incident, we always ate beside the train in a hurry and got back on as fast as we could to wait for the train to continue to our destination.

That was our trip to the border of Austria, making stops several times a day and running after the train at a moment's notice. By the time we got to the border we had eaten all of the food we took along and all we had left was the emergency money.

FRAUENDORF

We crossed the border and arrived in a little Austrian town called Frauendorf in Lower Austria close to Vienna, where the Mayor of the town was waiting for all evacuees from Yugoslavia. He walked us to the end of the village and gave us a small schoolhouse with a couple of rooms where we could live until the war came to an end. The rest of the passengers on the train were told to go to other villages in that area but I can't remember the names of those villages. From the moment our army left us there, we were on our own waiting until they came back to tell us we could go back to the house we owned in Gross Betschkerek.

We were not welcome by the Austrian people, they called us bad people, Gypsies, and any other name you can imagine to degrade us. The Mayor told our neighbors to bring us something to eat, or at least that's how it seemed because they were not smiling or friendly when they knocked on our door to greet us and deliver their presents. Anyhow, each one of them tried to outdo the other by bringing us better meals and we were at least happy that we were together as a family and had food on our table. During our first night there, my grandmother was preparing the beds for us. To her surprise, as she was moving the straw mattresses she found onions inside. My mother got happy and said teasingly "that's good, now we have food that doesn't need to be cooked!" We all had a good laugh about it.

Every time we heard a train was coming from Gross Betschkerek, the five of us would walk to the train station to see if we could find anything out about my grandfather. After the second or third time of doing this, my mother and grandmother started to ask people getting off the train if anybody was from our city. Finally, a man asked us what we were inquiring about and he told us: "Don't think about going back there right now, wait until our army returns. Right now it's very dangerous. The Yugoslav-Partisans are searching for us; they have been killing many good people. There is a rumor that they arrested Herr Herman, the teacher from Kikinda. Do you know him? And Herr Doctor Janko, from Gross Betschkerek both of them were taken to the mill, along with many people that they have been taking away from their farms to torture and kill them, I guess, because I heard a lot of shooting from where I was hiding. Many times they only ask if you are German or German descendant, if the answer is affirmative, they will kill you in an instant, regardless of sex or age, including infants. There are groups of men and women that belong to the Partisan party who are thirsty for blood. I saw them yesterday surrounding the city from block to block, capturing boys, girls, pregnant women, beating them all up until they bled, then, taking them naked across the street to be shot in the head."

"Do you know Ernst Frey?" Katharina asked.

"The shoe maker from Lemandorf?"

"Yes, he is my husband, have you seen him?"

"When he saw that the Partisans were surrounding the block where he lived he locked the door. Later, several Partisans knocked the door down and ran in pointing their guns and shooting. He had hung himself from a rope in the attic."

The train was leaving, so our narrator ran to catch the caboose. We started to cry because of what he had told us. We doubted whether to believe him or not, but we wept all the way home. We thought that Ernst was sure that he was going to be captured, tortured and killed; maybe that was why he took such determination on his life. This man had also told us that when the Partisans found my grandfather, they dragged him out of the house and just threw him on the other side of a fence in a cemetery located across the street from where he was living. That was the story we heard about our grandfather. We never found out where or if they buried him.

A few weeks after our arrival in Frauendorf a farmer stopped by to offer my mother a job in his kitchen in exchange for some food. Even though the job didn't pay any schillings at all, when she came back from her first day of work, she was smiling because she was able to provide us with food, which my grandmother cooked for the family.

THE END OF WORLD WAR II

After living in Frauendorf for about one year, things started to get worse. I don't know who or for what reason, but there were airplanes flying so low that bullets were hitting the windows. The Americans, who were protecting Frauendorf, repelled with gunfire. From our house on the hilltop we could see that the Americans had over twenty cannons aiming towards the sky on the other side of the hill. Sometimes we were attacked from one to three times a day, other days we weren't attacked at all. When there was time, an alarm would sound and everybody would run to the bunker for protection. The last person in would close the heavy steel doors. At that point, darkness was our nightmare. We heard the machine guns, roaring airplanes and cannon bombs coming from the outside, mixed with cries from children and women screaming inside the bunker. It was scary as hell! I recall hearing a man trying to calm his wife, while I was effortlessly trying to calm my sisters and myself. We were trembling with fear, sobbing, while our mother and grandmother where trying to protect us from behind, trying to hold back their emotions. I can't remember how long we stayed in the only place that gave us shelter during the raids. When they attacked by surprise there was no time to run to the bunker, so we had to hide any place we could or get down on the ground facing down, trembling and crying.

On the least expected day, there was a profound calm. Word spread around that the war was over. A man was running along the streets of Frauendorf screaming with happiness that the war was over. Ladies opened the windows looking for airplanes in the sky not believing him. They started screaming at their neighbors in excitement, repeating over and over that the war was over. It was like a party, I had never before seen so many people out in the streets and full of happiness.

From our house, we could see down below several streets and all the commotion and cheering that was going on. Naturally, we joined in everybody's happiness but my grandmother told us not to go out. No one in town was as happy as we were that the war had ended. I overheard my mother and grandmother talking about going back home and being reunited with our father, about whom we had received news recently that he was alive and well and still fighting.

The Americans stayed in town for several months after the end of The Second World War. They were happy too; they were talking about returning to America. Soldiers wandered around town while people greeted and congratulated them with joy. Every person in town smiled at them and we were all grateful for the protection they had given us against the communists.

MY FIRST KISS

My grandmother was so enthusiastic in those days that she started to bake cookies for my sisters and me. I helped her, hoping to get the baking pot and eat the remains of the bake. A group of American soldiers passed in front of our house and for some reason they returned and came inside without asking if they could. They started talking to us and we assumed they asked what was in the oven, because we didn't speak any English. My grandmother answered, willingly offering cookies, and asking them to wait for a little while. When the cookies were ready, she gave me a tray and told me to offer the warm cookies to the American soldiers. I went up to them smiling and saying "bitte?" "bitte?" They jumped over to take as many as they pleased. The last soldier was a man much older then the others, he took what was left and looking into my eyes gave me a kiss on the cheek saying, "Bist ein suesses Maedchen" (you are a sweet girl). It seemed to me that he must have been a family man and father of a girl about my age and as gracious as I was. After a few days of this incident, I thought to myself *Oh, that was my first kiss from somebody who was not a member of my family!*

FILIP

Filip, a relative of ours, and his family came to Frauendorf to look for us. He came from another town where he and his family had been taken to live, somewhere in Austria. He was married to Magda who was my mother's cousin. Filip was also German-Yugoslavian born in Rudolfsgnad, Yugoslavia where he owned a knitting factory. He was very happy because the war was over and had come to Frauendorf to take us back home. My grandmother was waiting for her son Ernst to come back from the war, the last she'd heard from him was that he had become an engineer designing bridges and he was on his way home. My mother had been waiting for my father Adam to come and get us, but had just found out that my father was a prisoner of war. They were afraid to go back home because they had no idea what the situation was in Gross Betschkerek or what they were going to get into, and hesitated on what to do. Since Filip was a man and was related to the family, when he told us we should go back to Gross Betschkerek, we all followed him.

GOING BACK HOME

We got ready to leave Frauendorf. We packed our belongings in a hurry and walked three blocks to the train station. We didn't have any Austrian friends or any people to say farewell to us, "The Gypsies," or wish us good luck on our way to the border of Subotica, Yugoslavia. We just followed uncle Filip, who did not know what had been happening in our homeland, nor had he investigated the situation before we got to the border.

At the time, none of us had any idea what was really happening. It wasn't until years later that I learned that at the beginning of the war, our army had left Gross Betschkerek promising to return in a couple of weeks to regain control of Yugoslavia, but because of the war, they were never able to come back. Now that the war had ended, Yugoslavia was under the control of powerful Guerrilla so-called Partisans led by Josip Broz Tito and the Soviet Union.

To our surprise, as soon as we got off the train in Subotica, Communist Yugoslav-Partisans ordered all the passengers aboard our train to get off and make groups according to nationalities. Germans in one group, Hungarians, Croatians, Jews, Gypsies and many other nationalities I can't remember, in other groups. Just before they transferred us to another train, they began to search everyone and their belongings.

From the moment we had left Gross Betschkerek, my grandmother had been carrying with her about eight dress suits and several pairs of shoes and many other personal things that belonged to her son Ernst, who had been enlisted in the German

Army. Before they searched us, she started to give them away to any man that she thought might fit into them, afraid that the soldiers would take them away from her. She was saving those items for Ernst's return home from the war, but would rather give them away then to have the Serbian Communists take them from her. When it was our turn to get searched, they took some of our clothes away and let us keep only the ones they decided we would need where we were going. Naturally, we also grabbed as many of our valuables as we were allowed.

Uncle Filip was taken away from us. We later found out that he and his family were taken to a concentration camp called Gakovo in Yugoslavia. All I can remember about his children is that their names were Walter and Grete. I remember Grete as a baby girl since she was the same age as my sister Gertrude. Grete died of malnutrition in the Gakovo concentration camp in January of 1946.

The Communist Partisans ordered us to get into another train, hushing us with their guns while pushing us into an animal wagon. They kept forcing more people in, and it just got more and more crowded making it hard to breathe. The children and the elderly managed to sit on the wooden floor, while the rest had to ride standing up. We had no idea where they were taking us or for what reason.

KRUSCHEVLJE

As it turned out, we were taken to a concentration camp for German-Yugoslavians. The camp was called Kruschevlje and it was located in Yugoslavia close to the Hungarian border between Subotica and Kikinda, so it did not take long to get there from where we were. Kruschevlje was a German village that had two rows of houses, one in front of the other, with a street in between, surrounded by a shallow ditch. It was watched over by groups of soldiers day and night. I didn't know this at the time, but Kruschevlje had been converted into a concentration camp for the sole purpose of annihilating German-Yugoslavians. A place to get rid of the people they didn't think worthy of living. We would soon find out that the only way out of there was if the bastard Partisans killed us, if we died of malnutrition or if we did everything we could to survive.

At our arrival, all of the houses were empty. It seemed to me that these houses had belonged to rich Germans, but their inhabitants were no longer there. Just like our hometown, this small village had also been evacuated or forced to move who knows where. Aside from the soldiers, we were the only ones who would occupy the camp now. We had no idea we would suffer all of the illness, death, torture and unimaginable inhumane things they would do to us for their own enjoyment.

The Partisan communist soldiers who guarded that concentration camp ordered us to make a single file line in order to search us. Lucky for us, since my sisters and I were so small and didn't move very fast, we ended up towards the back of the line. From there, we saw what was happening to people up ahead and could somehow prepare ourselves for what was coming. We saw many people walk past us crying and holding their ears in pain. We heard them saying that the soldiers were searching everything, yanking jewelry with force and without any warning, just ripping them off people's earlobes, necks and fingers. Just like that! I'm sure if they had a hard time pulling someone's ring from their finger they wouldn't have hesitated to chop the person's finger off. I heard a man complaining that they had beaten him up using their long guns because he had tried to stop them from taking his wife's earrings.

While we stood in line, my mother managed to hide her wedding ring and pictures of our family as they were the only things of value she had left; my grandmother hid her pearl-clip. My sisters wore no jewelry. I took off my gold ring and put it in my mouth, my earrings and ruby chain too. When it was our turn to get searched, my mouth had already started to fill with saliva making my cheeks look like balloons about to explode. Afraid of being caught, I didn't spit. I kept quiet trying not to tremble or call any attention to myself. I was terrified! I couldn't speak or swallow. Since I was a little girl maybe they didn't look at me too closely. They didn't find anything worthy of taking from us except for the few clothes the Partisan soldiers had let us keep when we had left Subotica. After we passed the inspection we were left wearing only the clothes we had on. They took everything we owned except for the few things we had managed to hide.

The house assigned to us had many rooms. Our room was to be shared with about twenty other German-Yugoslavians. The rest of the rooms in the house held about the same number of people in each room. On the floor of each room there was straw from wall to wall with only a narrow path in the center.

You could sit down, lie down or stand up on your straw bed. It was too crowded to do anything else. There was no privacy at all. The only furniture in the house was in the so-called dining room which had a few stools, some chairs and a table. I don't know if the other people we were sharing the room with were related to each other, but they were strangers to us.

When I felt safe to do so, I spat out the jewels in my hands along with a mouthful of saliva, saying "here mom." My mother and grandmother were surprised. My mother scolded me saying, "what would've happened if the soldiers had found you smuggling those jewels from them?" She took them from me and saved them with care, not knowing that those jewels would later be our way to freedom.

At nightfall, there was complete darkness all over the village. We were all starving after a day of traveling without eating or drinking water. We were irritated because of what was happening to us, children were crying, we were depressed, thirsty, terrified because of the complete darkness. We had some problems finding our own bed in the dark, but that never caused any trouble among our strange roommates since all of us respected each other's space. Soon we all got used to our new surroundings and knew how to get to our own bed with no problem at all, even in the dark. On that first night, as we tried to accommodate our bodies to our new beds, we couldn't help but be disgusted with uncle Filip! We were not alone in our distress, people started to complain and were very upset, not yet realizing or understanding what was really happening to us. My sisters and I fell asleep resting assured that our mother and grandmother would protect us.

Sunrise came and we all started to go out of our rooms to familiarize ourselves with our new environment. There were no instructions or anyone to show us around Kruschevlje or tell us where we could find food; we were very hungry and upset. A long line of people in the yard in front of a door indicated to us where the bathroom was, I mean "the hole," with a dirty wood board where you had to sit to release your daily needs. We missed our home, our bathroom with a carpet-decorated board and other commodities left behind. There was also a water well in the back yard of each house with a wooden bucket hanging from a rope. People staying in the same house as us started to get water from the well to cleanse themselves and their families. Everyone was perplexed; some complained loudly as if that would solve the problem about things left back home. Things like a private bedroom to sleep in with a nice comfortable bed; a bathroom with warm water to bathe in; a room to undress; a living room; a dining room; all those things we used for every day living were now missing from our lives in the blink of an eye.

The City Hall was used as the main quarters for the Serbian Partisan officers; there was another big house that was used by the soldiers as a dorm, with a big kitchen and plenty of rooms with beds to accommodate them. The storeroom had plenty of food to last them through the war they were fighting or revolution they had created in Yugoslavia. There was no food for us captives or stores to buy it in. Even if there had been, it's not like we had money to buy a piece of bread. Anything of little value had been taken away from us.

Some women had found the kitchen and started cooking or maybe they were only warming water to clean their children with a damp rag, because I don't remember the smell of food cooking or even coffee that morning. The water from the well was our breakfast! The quiet morning of our first day at Kruschevlje was interrupted by the sound of a drum coming from the distance. We all turned to see where the sound was coming from and saw some soldiers approaching us yelling and ordering us to go to the soccer field on the other side of the village.

They had us form a long line, grabbed a few young boys by their shirts and pushed them around ordering them back to the village. They pointed at some young women ordering them to follow a soldier back to camp; then yelled and pushed some more people around, pointing with their guns toward their quarters. We were all afraid of being taken who knows where or why. Another soldier flung some wooden buckets to some young fellows pointing to the water well and then to their quarters, talking in one of the local languages.

Before they left, they barked at us that soon we would eat some breakfast. My mouth was watering thinking I would be drinking coffee with bread. They started walking away, laughing and looking at each other as if mocking us and left us standing right there where we were. When people started to ask where their family members had been sent, the soldiers' faces turned to stone and they didn't bother responding, pointing their guns at them to shut them up.

Later the same day, they came back with the drummer again. They ordered us to line up and gave us a bowl that we would use to eat our only daily meal for as long as we were at the concentration camp in Kruschevlje. This would be our routine if we managed to survive hunger, malnutrition, unhealthy living conditions of life in general, lack of medicine and soap, and most of all if we were lucky enough not to be killed by the miserable bastards.

The young boys came back in the afternoon carrying food to be distributed among all of us. This would be used by the women to cook our barley soup or "meal of the day" if one could call it that. The soup was always cooked with bugs floating in it. Every day we were forced to eat the same barley soup with bugs. Being hungry is one of the most terrible things that can happen to a human being. Many of us refused to eat that food, at least during the first couple of days. After that, we ate anything, regardless of what it was or if anything was floating in it. Every fifteen days or so, a single piece of bread of about 8 inches long and 2 inches wide was given to us to be distributed among ten people. It was as hard as a rock. There was always a big argument every time it had to be cut into ten pieces of the same size.

The young men who were assigned to carry water every day to both quarters were gone practically the whole day and didn't come back until the afternoon. The captive women and young girls who had to cook, do the laundry, do the cleaning, and of course serve the Partisan pigs came back after dark. From that moment on, we understood that any one of us could be forced to work, like it or not.

SOLD AS SLAVES

The Serbian Communists returned again before noon with the same drummer, ordering us to get out of our assigned houses. They pointed to a woman that was standing beside her mother and her three children; both the woman and her mother protested. In response they were beaten up, with the older woman being left on the floor recovering from pain. The Communist Serbians pointed at seven more women who were all taken to officer quarters along with the first woman they had pointed at. The captives were in complete disarray. They argued among each other, but that was all they could do, talk and complain.

That same afternoon the eight women returned accompanied by soldiers to say good-bye to their families. They were crying while they hugged their children. The ingrates rushed them outside, and began to load them onto a truck. As this was happening, the beaten up old lady from early in the morning was crying desperately, pleading to the soldiers not to take her daughter away from her and her three children. She rushed over to her daughter and embraced her as if protecting her with her own body. As a result, she was beaten once again and left on the soiled ground, crying and asking God for mercy. The three children kneeled around her, not understanding anything of what was happening to their mother or grandmother. Hours later, she got up still crying and sobbing as the captives around her tried to comfort her.

A few days later, she was nowhere to be found. The little ones wandered alone around camp crying and hungry. A woman hugged them and tried to console them, hoping the grandmother would return. Then I remember a big commotion around our water well. There were a lot of people trying to look deep down the opening. My mother did not allow us to go and see what was happening, but I remember the rumor being that the old woman had killed herself by jumping down our well. From that point on, the water was boiled as that was the only water supply for our house and it would have been impossible to live without drinking any water. When all resources for making fire were no longer available around camp, we had no other choice but to drink the water or die of dehydration. Many times that was all we had for breakfast, lunch or supper. We never heard or knew the whereabouts of the eight women after they were taken.

Among the captives at Kruschevlje were children, teenagers, elderly people and young men and women; there were married couples with children as well as single people. There weren't that many men at the campsite as the German Army had drafted most of them. The few men that had not been drafted for one reason or another, as well as boys, were forced to do hard labor or were sold as slaves.

Now there was no doubt in our minds, we were captives being held against our will at a concentration camp simply for being born German-Yugoslavian. It did not make a difference nor did it help us that my father had served the Yugoslavian army. We were forced to live in a concentration camp. We were free, as long as we didn't try to escape. There were soldiers walking all over the concentration camp watching us day and night. The Serbian Communists were doing to us what our soldiers had done to the Jews and other people during WWII. To them, our lives were worthless and they didn't want us alive. We all had to fight for survival, no matter what or how.

No one knew exactly where Kruschevlje was located until a few days after we had been taken there, when five old men from the concentration camp were talking behind our house. One of them spoke to the others, pointed with his finger, and said, "By walking in that direction for about an hour or so would get us to the border of Hungary where our freedom is waiting for us, if any of us are willing to take a chance." I looked in the direction where he was pointing, and then turned to look at him. No one said a word. All of them were looking at the open field the old man had been talking about, with no houses or trees to hide behind as far as the eye could see. Most of the soldiers were guarding that side of the camp.

Another old man interrupted their thoughts by saying, "about eighty of us died of hunger yesterday…about the same the day before…and today more than…" I didn't wait for him to finish his sentence. I grabbed both of my sisters by their hands and pulled them making them run with me. I was so scared! We didn't stop running until we found our grandmother who was cooking our only meal at the common kitchen along with other women. We stayed by her side and didn't let go of one another. I only remember a feeling of panic had come over me. We were not allowed to go into the soldiers' quarters, where my mother was working for our captors.

BEGGARS

It didn't take long before we all became beggars, otherwise we would have died of malnutrition. Soon we realized that we could go begging almost any place we liked, even to the closest small villages outside of the concentration camp. The only villages no one dared to go begging in were the ones in the direction of Hungary since there were more soldiers watching over that side of the camp. At the beginning we didn't know we were risking our lives every time we walked out of camp to go begging. At the soldiers' wishes, our food could be searched or taken away from us, or even thrown away, depending on the state of mind or mood that the bastards were in. One of the first things we learned at the camp was not to make eye contact with the enemy, or else you could end up dead, beaten or punished in whatever manner they decided to use. We were at their merciless thoughts, whether immoral, criminal, or evil. The soldiers knew that even if we left, we had our mothers waiting for us and women had their children or parents at camp. We would feel forced to come back every time we went to the village to beg for a piece of hard corn bread or anything else we could get.

One day, about five adults and fifteen children and teenagers went to the closest village, me along with them. I didn't ask my mother if I could go because many other young girls were also going, besides, I was starving more than ever that morning. When we got there, we all split up and went begging all day long. By the afternoon, three of us decided to go back to camp together, happy because good-hearted people had given us hard corn bread and plenty of other food we could eat and share with our families. As it turned out, luck was on my side that day, or at least that's how I see it now looking back. As we made our way back to camp, two pigs caught us and made us go to their quarters with the pretext that they had to search us. They pushed my two friends and me into the front yard against a high brick wall and made us put our hands up against the wall. As we stood there we realized that we weren't alone. There were several other kids standing there with their hands up against the wall too. I recognized them because they had gone begging with us that day. They were now in the same predicament as us. Standing behind us were several evil soldiers with mounted guns. I could see that the wall was splattered with old blood and its pungent smell was nauseating. We all stood there shaking and crying wondering what the soldiers were planning to do with us. I could hear that my friends, who had been taken to an adjoining room, were crying and yelling for help. At that moment a pig came running into the yard shouting something about an approaching vehicle. All of a sudden the Serbian soldiers started running around nervously; it looked like they didn't know what to do and pushed us away from the brick wall rushing us into the street. I ran as fast as I could and didn't stop until I found my mother and gave her my booty. She asked me if everything was ok, and even though I nodded my head yes, my shaking body betrayed me. She asked me not to go begging any more, she didn't like us to beg and besides she would be devastated if something were to happen to any of us.

Working in the kitchen of the bastard pigs was one of the jobs women tried to get, because even though the soldiers kept an eye on them constantly, the women managed to smuggle potato peels and any other vegetable remains they could get. Some females managed to take home the garbage from the quarters of the spurious pigs. When they would get home they would quickly sift through the garbage in the hopes of finding something edible. If they were lucky, among all the garbage they would find a bone with a tiny piece of meat or fat on it, or sometimes a chewed piece of meat. If they found any empty potato rucksacks, they would keep them for when they went begging. Other captives would go behind the soldiers' quarters to pick up any remains the soldiers may have thrown on the ground back there. Any of that garbage, even bones, was a banquet to us. Otherwise we would have starved to death with our once a day soup.

When there was no wood to cook, we ate the remains that my mother smuggled from the kitchen with a little salt. If you are hungry you eat anything. I remember biting little by little the peel of a carrot or potato with a bit of salt. Even though some people were shot to death, raped or punished for garbage smuggling, being hungry or hearing the cries of young children or infants asking for food was enough for any of these women to take a chance and do it over and over again. If not, we ate what we got from begging. We missed badly all the things we took for granted before we were brought to the concentration camp like coffee, meat, chocolate, cookies...

Early one morning, there was the damned drummer again which meant we had to go outside to hear what they wanted. They passed our house and kept on going almost to the last house to our right. The soldiers entered that house abruptly and pulled out a man and a boy, beating them with their guns and kicking them. They fell on the ground and the soldiers started to punch them. They pushed them against a wall and shot them dead. Just like that! We were shocked to see such a criminal act. They walked away as if nothing had happened! We could not do anything to save our own lives, much less that of our neighbors. Afraid to run the same luck we all kept our mouths shut. No one knew why the man and boy had been killed.

EMMY

At the camp, we had a roommate named Emmy whose straw bed was beside ours. She was about twenty-four years old and a good-looking, well-mannered young woman who spoke with grace and was very polite. She had a four-year-old son named Herbert.

One day in 1946, Emmy and I left camp early in the morning to go begging. I cannot remember the exact date, but one thing I know for sure is that it was winter because it was snowing heavily. My mother was working for the mentally retarded pigs and my sisters were crying for food. All we could do was tighten a belt or something around our bellies to keep from feeling hungry. That morning Emmy had asked my grandmother if she could take care of Herbert while she went begging to the nearest village. When I asked if I could go too, my grandmother said no even though I kept insisting. There were at least ten other people that planned to go begging that day. Some of them said they had gone several times before and assured my grandmother that it would be safe, so she finally agreed to let me go.

After begging all day long, we could barely close our rucksacks since we had stuffed them with all the scraps the generous people from the villages had given us. My load was heavy. Emmy told me that we should wait until at least ten o'clock that night to head back to the camp to avoid being captured. So, we waited as long as we could. By the time we decided to start going back, the field was all white from the snow but the temperature wasn't too bad and the moon was full and bright. Even though it was nighttime, far ahead of us we saw a dark shadow that appeared to be up in the air. We had no idea what it could be, but it didn't give us the impression of being a threat to us. To our surprise it was one of the Serbian pigs riding a white horse. The white horse had fooled us, which was the reason we hadn't hidden from him. It was too late now. He asked us questions like where were we heading, etc. We answered him. He tried to whip us, but because of the tall horse he couldn't reach us. The soldier ordered us to follow him to a house at the entrance of camp.

As soon as he dismounted he told me to sit on a bench and he threw our rucksacks on the floor. He pushed Emmy hard against a wooden door. She complained politely. When the door opened, he pushed her inside violently. Emmy cried out loudly. I heard several men jeering loudly inside. I stayed there on that bench trying to make up my mind whether to take my food and leave or stay right there. If I ran away they could easily catch up to me. So I stayed. The door was closed so I could hardly hear my friend shouting and insulting them inside. She started to scream hysterically. I got curious and reached to the window to look inside. She was thrown on the wooden floor; a pig was holding her arms while two more held her legs apart. On top of her, between her legs, was the horse rider with his pants down to his knees and his ass was moving up and down. Then they changed places, not paying any attention to her pleads. She was out of her mind, calling them names she wouldn't have dared before. The rider put a piece of iron with a triangular end in the fire. The evil men laughed at her suffering.

Another animal ripped her dress off to expose her breasts; a beast got between her legs and she started to scream again. She was desperate, pleading, begging for God's sake to be left alone. They only made fun of her pleads and enjoyed their actions. At the time, I had no idea why or what they were doing to her. With a slap on her face she was thrown to the floor again, forced to spread her legs once more. The wicked rider took the red iron out of the fire, walked to meet my poor friend and burned her on her genitals. She screamed, and screamed and screamed, kicking trying to free herself from them. Smoke came out from between her legs. I was frightened, but couldn't move from the window until I saw they were dragging her out. She was thrown out like an animal. I ran and kneeled beside my friend. I asked if she needed help, but she didn't answer me, just stayed there muffling and crying continuously. Finally she mumbled:

"Let's go; let's go. If I can't walk I'll crawl. I have to get to my Herbert…let's go before they come back."

"What happened, Emmy? What happened…? Can I help you? Tell me what I can do to help you?" I felt pity for her and started to cry.

"You…are too young to understand what happened in there…Let's go back. I don't think I can walk…let's go before they come and get me again…please…reach my rucksack…"

I handed her rucksack to her and she grabbed it and started to crawl. I walked beside her and she was crawling and dragging her rucksack. We went on crying. I walked slowly, trembling with fear, thinking that they could also get me and do terrible things to me. I feared of the unknown torture they could cause.

My grandmother and mother had been concerned waiting for us. They kept on asking me if something had happened to me, then asked Emmy. She didn't answer. Some women helped her get inside to her straw bed.

"Where is my baby? My son! Where is my baby?" she asked desperately.

When she found him, she cried and cried as she hugged him tenderly, kissing and talking to him with love. She kept crying softly. All of a sudden, she fainted.

My mother kept me in her arms all night long. I couldn't stop crying, tormented by my own secret, afraid that if I said anything they would kill me or do something terrible to me, as they had done to poor Emmy. During the next four days, Emmy kept getting fevers and chills on and off and suffered from cold sweats and nightmares. One of our roommates took care of her during that time, while my grandmother took care of Herbert.

I was a child who had witnessed a crime that winter night, not really knowing what had actually happened. Dreadful of telling even my own mother, keeping it as a secret buried deep inside my mind without being able to forget poor Emmy screaming with horror and anger, the red iron bar smoking. For many years I couldn't figure out what had happened to her, what I had seen, what those possessed animals…perverts…I just couldn't find a word that described that bunch of mad bastard communists!! *Die schweinehunden* (the pig dogs)!!! What had they done to our lives?!

From that night on, I had recurring nightmares about what they had done to Emmy, listening to her screams. I still experience the scenes of that frightful unforgivable winter night of 1946. As I grew up, I was able to understand the meaning of rape, and little by little had pictured in my mind what they were doing to that unfortunate woman; I never dared to tell or talk to anyone about it in my entire life, not even my mother. I endured my memories alone, until now. I pray to God to keep all mad communists burning in hell, over and over and over, for eternity!

The next day, very early in the morning, we heard the damned drummer again. They were coming in our direction. All of us looked at the ground or some other place, but never directly at the soldiers, if they talked to us, it was better not to make eye contact.

My mother had the impression they were coming to get Emmy and us too, for helping her. As they approached the five of us got together trying uselessly to protect each other. My legs weakened fearfully. The pigs stopped two houses from ours. They entered several other houses yelling, pushing and kicking people around. Several men were conducted to the officers' quarters. Then the drummer started coming in our direction again. I was so scared my body was shaking and I was just waiting for them to seize me or beat me to death. I gripped my mother's legs as hard as I could and before I realized, pee started running down my legs. It was a relief when I saw them pass in front of us and not even look at me. They stopped far away and kept grabbing more men and women and flinging them to the ground, using the same method as many times before.

The reason these captives were being arrested was to punish them because they hadn't obeyed orders to do hard labor at the cemetery; they were asked to take their clothes off in front of all the inhabitants of Kruschevlje. Once naked, they were forced to get into a basement full of water. The punishment consisted of spending twenty-four hours in the water filled basement. Winter or summer, autumn or spring, the Serbian soldiers administered this form of punishment not caring what season of the year it was.

THE MASSACRE

On another occasion, several children and some adults were returning to the concentration camp from a day of begging, *die schweinehunden* had captured some of them, while others made it home safely. The next day, we heard the damned drummer again. That drummer was bad news all the time. Our legs shook every time we heard the pigs marching around camp at the pace of the damned drummer. So we all walked outside to hear what they had to tell us. All I remember was seeing some of my friends, several young women and two old men standing by a wall, and one of the pigs started yelling:

"This is a warning to all of you! Keep it in mind so you learn not to go begging any more! This is what's going to happen to you if you insist on going out of this camp!" The drummer started to beat his drum, stopped abruptly and a retard yelled "Fire!!"

The sound of gunfire made us jump. Women screamed in horror! Men yelled and called them names with anger. Children started crying frightened. I just couldn't believe what was happening right in front my eyes. Was I having a nightmare? I looked again toward the wall where they were laying on the ground, most were dead, and some were still shaking in agony. Their family members ran to the wall to check on their loved ones and tried lifting them as if trying to bring them to life. There were mothers screaming loudly for their children, husbands for their wives, wives for their husbands, while the assassins pointed toward all of us with their guns as they backed away toward their quarters as if nothing had happened. The bodies would remain in front of the wall where they had been assassinated until the next day.

We were all crying in horror. My grandmother and my mother protected us three with their arms, hiding our faces with their dresses. They didn't want us to see the blood of our own people splashed on the wall, running down the surface like a stream of red water. After that day, my sister Kathy sucked her thumb even more than before, while at the same time twirling her hair with her index finger. My mother tried to take her thumb out of her mouth using some force, but her face would get distorted with a look of terror, her eyes almost looked like they were going to pop out, and she would start crying and screaming out of control. The only way to calm her down was to let her keep sucking her thumb. She continued doing that for some years after the assassins had massacred our people in front of us.

There is no way I can forget these dreadful episodes of my life, especially that massacre in Kruschevlje. I've had many nightmares about that day. When I wake up, I can smell the vomit, excrement and urine of the frightened people that witnessed those horrible murders just as vividly as when they happened.

A horse-drawn carriage arrived at the concentration camp at least twice a week to pick up any dead bodies from the infirmary. The infirmary was a room where the communists kept the ill. In the room there were only a few straw beds for ill people to rest in. No one knew if the pigs ever really took care of the sick people, gave them any medicine or if a doctor or nurse saw them or took care of them. If any of the people in the infirmary died, the pigs ordered a few of the captives to pile the dead bodies in the horse-drawn carriage and made them go dig a hole in the cemetery to bury the dead in a common resting place. On the day after the killing, the carriage would have to take the slaughtered bodies in addition to the ones from the infirmary. The Serbians pointed at some women and boys to lift the corpses and pile them one over the other in the cart. As the carriage made its way over to the cemetery, some more people were told to follow along. Once they got to the cemetery, the people were ordered to make a common hole in the frosted soil to bury all the bodies in the same place.

FREEZING WINTER

There was plenty of wood to cook, at least for the first few weeks after imprisonment started. I think the Germans had that wood for their own use and when they were ordered to leave Kruschevlje, they had no other option but to leave it behind. Once that wood was gone, captives went out to the field looking for anything they could use to make a fire for cooking and heating our rooms. There weren't any trees around the camp, just plain fields several kilometers around with a few bushes here and there. Some captives started to use the wood from the few fences they could find and every family started to save any logs, wood chips or anything that could be used to make a fire. The warmth from the kitchen stove was enough to keep our rooms at a nice temperature during the winter. Unlike us, the Partisan bastards had plenty of logs for their own use.

The kitchen was big enough for all the families living in the house, but a lot of conflicts started when the logs or wood chips became scarce. Big arguments started over simple things such as a piece of wood or the use of the stove even though it was big enough to be shared by more than one family at a time. One night, a man had left a little piece of smoked ham hanging from a string above his bed. Since his bed was close to the window, someone stole his ham and the next morning he couldn't even find the string. He was upset and made a big deal about it. People started to talk about the incident of the little piece of smoked ham and wondered who had taken it. They began to lose trust in each other, even more so after the theft occurred.

As wood got limited, logs became very precious and some people hid them in secret places. It became a matter of life or death during the crude winter months since no one had anything to cover up with except their own worn off clothes. Everyone would calculate how many logs it would take to heat up water to cleanse themselves or make a soup of vegetable remains. No one seemed to want to share his or her fire with anyone else. This started to be a serious problem and the cause of many arguments. But as I said before, eventually it got to a point where there was no burning wood or anything that could be used for that purpose. We all started looking for anything that could be burned to make a fire.

As cold weather arrived, each family bundled up around the straw beds keeping us children in the middle, as that was the only way to keep warm during the cold winter nights. When any of our roommates died or were killed, we all got ready to take anything they had that could be of any use to us; even the straw from their beds was used to cover ourselves with on winter nights. The lack of burning materials was the cause of suspicion among all the adults at the German-Yugoslavian prison camp. Maybe they thought their roommates were going to steal the few burnable items they had left. Having a source of fire meant life or death for children and old people, who were easily dying of upper respiratory infections.

One winter morning, there was a man looking for something to burn. Some of our people had hidden wood so they could use it at a later time. Wood was saved as a treasure to be used, especially during the coldest nights. So, this old man found some hidden wood, and naturally, started to dig it out. When he managed to get it, it was covered with soil. While he was taking the soil off he started to swear very angrily. He carried the pieces of wood home, complaining that he found them inside a hole in the soil covered with human shit. He was wondering how our own people could do that.

When there were no more wood chips or wooden fences to burn in the kitchen, we started using the little bit of furniture we had around us. Chairs, tables, stools and benches became our firewood, even if it meant we had to eat sitting on the floor or standing up. Soon, even the doors from the inside of the house had disappeared. After those doors were burned, we could no longer feel the warmth of the kitchen in our rooms since there was nothing left to burn. We burned everything except our straw beds. After that winter and the next to come, we ate our meals cold, except for the barley soup that was cooked by our women in the kitchen at the main quarters. We cuddled tighter together to be able to make it from the beginning to the end of the glacial winter.

LICE INFESTATION

Because of the unhealthy conditions we were living in, plagues, infestations and skin diseases were very common. During the winter, without warm water it was impossible to keep the children clean. It wasn't like in the summer time when children and babies were bathed in cold water under the warm shining sun. There was no perfume or soap. The only way to cleanse our bodies was with a damp cloth. This was only when the weather was good, because during the winter months there wasn't much we could do and we walked around smelling like garbage.

All of a sudden, we were mercilessly attacked by a lice infestation. When we woke up one morning, our mother noticed that we kept scratching our heads. When she took a closer look, she was upset and said, "Oh my God! Why is this happening to us? What else are we expecting from this useless war! Look at this mother! Look at my three girls!"

Hundreds of lice were laying eggs in our hair. Immediately both of them asked us to sit on the floor in front of them while they started to hunt them, separating hair by hair, pulling the little insects with their nails, while we complained they were pulling our hair.

The guards gave mothers scissors and razor blades to shave their children's heads and also adults. Dealing with the pests by shaving their children's hair almost to the scalp was not a smart solution. My mother didn't want to have to shave our hair. She was proud of our hair and loved the way our hair curled in a different way from each other. Kathy's curled the most, Gertrude's only a little and mine was less curly then Kathy's but more than Gertrude's. She was going to do whatever it took in order not to have to touch our hair.

After a week of battling the micro insects, the Serbian Communists gave all of us in Kruschevlje some kind of soap to rub on our scalps, which ended up being a good remedy for our own good and theirs too. We were glad to get rid of the plague.

KATHARINA

In the fall of 1946, even though my mother had sworn no one from her family would ever beg for food again, hunger took a toll on us and our only option was to start begging again. This included my mother, who felt a necessity to find food for her children, and did not care about the consequences of going or what could happen when she returned. The German-Yugoslavian captives ignored the warning the communists had given when they conducted the massacre in front of us all.

Some people went begging and were lucky to make it back safely; others weren't, whether they were women, children or elderly. I'm sure if God had dared to go begging out of Kruschevlje, He would have run the same danger we had. He might have gotten shot, tortured, raped or have suffered any number of other terrible things that had been done to our people.

My mother had no choice but to beg, leaving us under our grandmother's care. She stayed at the edge of camp, observing for an opportunity when the pigs were not paying attention. We saw her leaving from the concentration camp safely and heading towards the village after several hours of waiting and watching the bastards. Perhaps they had let her pass since they knew she would have to return.

She went begging from one house to another and asking bystanders on the street for anything they could spare. No one gave her anything, not even a crust of hard corn bread. Maybe all these good hearted people were tired of giving us small pieces of smoked bacon, bread, onions, potatoes, lard, an apple or a small amount of roast pork. After several hours of walking and asking around, she entered a grocery store and for some reason that I never asked, she exchanged her wedding band for a kilo of salt. I don't know if she gave her wedding band so she could prepare our food with a little flavor or why she had done it. Later on that same day, she found people much more generous. Once she returned, my mother would give us everything she received from begging in small pieces for us to chew or taste. Something like coffee was never given to us, let alone flour. Coffee was a luxury for our benefactors and flour was of no use to us. A spoonful of sugar or salt would have been like a present sent to us from heaven.

To this day, all the people from those blessed villages are in my prayers. God bless them all and keep them in heaven. Thanks to all of them and their relatives that are still alive. Without their help we would never have made it through those miserable days we spent thanks to the bastard Serbian Communists. I wish I could find a word in my vocabulary to offend those pigs as they all deserve.

At day's end, her arms were full with all the food she was able to collect so she started walking back to camp. She had to be very careful because if the pigs saw her carrying all those goods, she could end up dead, punished or raped, as had been the case for others. From far away she observed the entrance to Kruschevlje. For some reason, that day there were more soldiers walking around and going in and out of camp than usual, so she stayed in the open field hiding behind a few bushes. Several hours later, nothing had changed. As tired and thirsty as she was, she lied down on the soil and waited for the right moment to pass unnoticed into camp.

In the mean time, my grandmother was worried about my mother. As night approached she started to look from the window along the entrance of the concentration camp. By midnight she got desperate. At sunrise I found her standing in front of the main door, looking intently at the entrance of camp. All day long, she hadn't wanted to eat or drink any water. She was talking and talking about my mother, blaming her for what she had done. Angry at the damned pigs and the war. Wondering if there really existed a God, and if He existed, why He allowed all this to be happening. Why didn't He stop this war and our suffering? Later she asked us to pray for our mother. Some fellow roommates kneeled by their bed and prayed with us to Jesus and the Virgin Mary. I tried to stay awake by her side, but soon fell sound asleep.

On the second morning, my grandmother was talking louder and louder, she was saying things that didn't make any sense to me. I just couldn't understand what she meant. She wouldn't stop talking and ripping out her hair. She looked desperate. She kept walking out of the room, looking towards the edge of camp and talking louder. Going back indoors, kneeling and praying, sitting on the bed, then quickly getting up and running outside again to take a look.

Some of our roommates tried effortlessly to calm her down, telling her that my mother was fine, that all we had to do was wait a little longer; she would be back. That there were too many pigs around camp and that she must be hiding there, waiting for an opportunity to pass without being noticed. She just couldn't handle it any more; she lost control of herself and didn't let us go out. I was afraid. Kathy and Gertrude came to me and we hugged each other and prayed together for our mother and grandmother. Praying made us feel better or safer. Later that afternoon, my grandmother was completely out of her mind, pulling her clothes, messing up her hair, touching her face, talking loudly, shouting "GOD, PLEASE HELP HER!! BRING

HER BACK ALIVE!!" She wouldn't stop crying and pulling her hair.

My mother had been hiding and sleeping in the sparse bushes for three days, scared to be detected and worried for her mother and us. She was afraid to be shot or punished. To add to her anguish, a soldier found her and took her to a house in the outskirts of the concentration camp where several beggars had been captured. That was the same house where I had almost gotten shot. A few hours later, she and the others were told to stand against a wall to be executed. When she was about to get shot, a soldier recognized her as a worker in their kitchen and pulled her out of there letting her go safely into camp.

By the time my mother was able to get back, my grandmother was in complete shock and out of her mind. Our friends had taken her to the infirmary. As soon as my mother knew what happened to her mother, she went to the infirmary to see her, but the damned bastards did not allow her to see her until late the next day.

She told me many years later, with tears in her eyes, that when she was finally allowed to visit her mother she had hardly recognized her. She looked deformed and her hair was a mess, bloodstained from having pulled it from the roots. My mother got goose bumps all over her body at the sight of her mother. She also told me that she felt a knot in her throat and tears rolled out of her eyes from seeing her own mother so sick and in such distress. She wanted to hug her, talk to her, but couldn't because her mother was completely insane and didn't recognize her. My mother cried and felt so hurt when her mother pushed her away as she tried to hug her, screaming, desperately calling her names while continuing to pull her hair out.

She had refused to eat or drink. As undernourished as she had become, she passed away. There were no muscles in her skinny body, just bones covered by the only dress she had worn since we were made prisoners at Kruschevlje, just for being born German-Yugoslavians. I always wonder if she died or if the bastards had killed her. Surprisingly, they allowed us four to walk beside the heap of bodies on the funeral wagon. Only those who were mourning a member of their family were allowed to follow the long way from the concentration camp, through the soccer field and to the cemetery. Some of our fellow captives had been ordered to dig a grave before the funeral wagon got there. None of us were allowed to get close to our deceased relatives. The same captives who had dug the grave were told to bury my grandmother and some other deceased people. They carefully dropped her body, along with six other skeleton looking bodies, into the open ground where they still lay until resurrection. That was all that remained from our dead, skin and bones covered by rags, no muscles or any fat on them, you could count the ribs on each body.

AGAINST THEIR WILL

I can never forget all of the things that happened to me on one crude winter morning in January of 1947 when I was almost raped. Hunger made us do things we would never have thought of doing, or put ourselves in danger of being shot to death by our mentally ill guardians, or raped by sadistic soldiers or farmers taking advantage of defenseless children. Sometimes teenagers were beat up before they were raped, since the rapists knew no one was going to protect them.

We were worthless and vulnerable. We would've been better off freezing to death while walking out of camp then being raped or beat up and living with the memory. Being hungry is something dreadful. You will do anything or take any risk, including dying, for a piece of bread to mitigate your hunger, especially if there are crying children asking you for food.

I pray to God not to allow anything like that to happen to us ever again. After my experience at the camp, I promised myself I would never beg again for as long as I lived, and to this day, I never have and I thank God for it. No matter what happened, I never stopped working to be able to support myself and my family.

That cold morning I heard that some of my friends were going to beg at another village further away that was less guarded for a while. I can't bring to my memory the names of those small villages, where marvelous people used to live. I asked my mother if I could go but she said no because it was dangerous and she just couldn't think of what her life would be like if she lost one of her girls. My friends insisted saying that it was safe because they had found a way of returning without being detected. Finally she agreed to let me go.

Ah! That winter was getting colder. Our clothes were getting more and more useless for winter, my socks were long gone, my dress was ripped and coming apart at the seams and in order for me to go begging, my sister lent me her sweater. Her sweater was very small for me, but I forced myself in it. I needed it to cover at least my back and half of my arms. Clothes had become of great value at camp. Taking the clothes off of a dead body was not an act of stealing, it was a matter of survival. We needed them in order to cover our bodies from the cold and the wind. We all missed our coats that were taken away from us when we arrived in Kruschevlje. My shoes were practically gone. The soles had come apart, but I managed to keep the snow off my toes as much as I could by flapping them up as I walked. Many times I thought about fixing them by tying some string or a rag around them, but it would have been a miracle to find anything usable. The truth was that there was not a thread, piece of wire, rope or a rag in all Kruschevlje that I could have used to hold the soles together.

As we headed to the village to beg, there were five of us walking down a road, two girls about 15 to 17 years old, and two boys about 12, which is how old I was at the time. We tried not to talk too much since we had to be very aware of our surroundings, making sure we paid attention to who was coming and from where. We made sure to keep an eye out for the bastards so that they wouldn't catch us by surprise. Sometimes we would run with our arms crossed and our fingers under our armpits to keep them warm. Now thinking back I wonder if our noisy shoes could've been heard from far away.

Our goal was to get to a farm and ask the farmer if he would let us stay there overnight. That way we could get a fresh start the next day into the village, beg all day long and return home by midnight. Luckily, we found a farmer that agreed to let us stay and the five of us ran happily to sleep in the barn. We buried our bodies in the straw to get warm. In the middle of the night, two men came into the barn where we were sleeping. They pulled the two girls aside and the girls started to complain and asked the men to leave them alone. Then we heard them cry in pain and scream for help. We didn't know what to do or what they were doing to them. The boys just looked without knowing what was happening. I jumped to their side and we all embraced tightly, our bodies shaking with fear. It was dark, but once our eyes adjusted to the darkness, we could see a little bit. We remained motionless, as we were defenseless children in comparison to the grown up attackers.

I still have nightmares of this episode of my life; I wake up hearing their pleads, their cries, and the laughter of those miserable dogs who seemed to enjoy themselves even more when my innocent girlfriends were asking for mercy. When they were satisfied with my two friends, they looked at me. One asked the other what they were going to do with me. I started to tremble, more from fear than from the cold night. I did not have the slightest idea what they pretended to do to me. I knew it would be something frightful. I thought about my father, wished that he were there to protect me from those monsters. *Mother help me*, I pleaded over and over again in my mind, knowing that she was far away at camp, waiting for me to return. I was just about to get killed by two strangers! I wanted to see who they were—see their faces. I started to pray to God for protection. He must've heard my prayers because I understood what they were saying in Serbian:

"Leave her alone, don't bother with her, she is too skinny."

They left laughing happily and satisfied, sure that no one would tell them anything. We were worthless; nobody cared about what happened to us and there weren't any authorities to protect us. Even though there were many kind people who helped us or fed us, there were many others who were only ready to hurt us whenever they pleased. They were free to do whatever they wished to harm us, just for being young, weak or German descendants held captive and almost at death's door. I hope those spurious rapists who called themselves men are in hell, burning for being such stupid animals. Our friends stayed on the straw where the men had left them. They didn't dare move, ashamed and crying out of control. The three of us did not let go of each other, still trembling from the unknown danger. When the poor frightened girls looked for us, we all embraced together, hoping for those miserable animals not to come back later. I asked crying, "What happened? What did they do to you? Tell me please!" They just kept on crying, looking down, sobbing for the rest of the night.

Before sunrise we left and headed toward the village. We walked along the road, holding hands together until we reached the first few houses, hoping for a better day. Before nightfall we walked back to Kruschevlje, walking very slowly. The girls were ashamed and didn't say a word. The frigid weather was freezing our bones! We kept on walking down the road, flip flopping our shoes, looking to each other for comfort and protection. We took our time so that we would reach camp at midnight. We walked safe into camp with no problem. Sometimes I wonder why the communists hadn't been guarding the camp as before. Maybe their war was coming to an end or they noticed that there were not many of us left. I doubt it was because they had pity on us, because they were mad animals!

I proudly gave my mother my treasure, my day's work. Food was the most valuable wealth, besides our own lives. The generous people of the village gave me small pieces of smoked ham, homemade sausage, headcheese, a piece of liver sausage, three potatoes, an onion, bread and many other things that made my rucksack almost too heavy for the unhealthy girl I had become. That food would last us for at least a week, aside from our slimy, purple looking, odorless barley soup of the day. Once again, God bless those people who helped us to survive imprisonment.

When my mother found out what happened to my friends, she wept too. That had been the third time I had gone begging, and the last. She didn't permit me to go any more after that. At least not while we were still in custody at the concentration camp. Thank God she was always able to smuggle remains from the kitchen to mitigate our hunger.

MY JEWELS FOR FREEDOM

In the middle of January of 1947, the field was covered with snow as far as the eye could see. That was the crudest winter of my entire life. I will never forget it. It didn't help that our clothes, or I should say rags, were barely enough to keep the wind from freezing us to death.

My mother heard that we could buy our freedom by paying some willing guards to lead us from Kruschevlje to Hungary. It was a matter of life or death, our only options were to buy our freedom or to take our chances at Kruschevlje and possibly starve to death. That is why my mother decided to take a risk by using my gold ring, earrings and ruby chain that I had managed to smuggle into camp in exchange for our freedom. She knew it could be a trap, but it was a chance she decided to take in the hopes of getting us out of there once and for all.

The guards were only asking for some type of payment in return and didn't seem to care how they were paid or with what. The bastards knew we didn't have much left because they had taken most of our belongings from us. They also knew that there were some precious belongings we all managed to hide from them. This time they were not stealing our jewelry, they were allowing us to use it to pay for our freedom. Those guards would guide our way but they would not be there to help those who couldn't make it all the way through. We had to be sure to follow them no matter what, because if we stayed behind for any reason whatsoever, we would be on our own. We could freeze to death and no one would be there to help the weak.

The word spread that every person who wanted to go had to be at the edge of camp way before daybreak. That would be our departure point to freedom. Most of the prisoners gathered there, nervous, quiet, waiting and waiting. Afraid of the soldiers, but they said nothing to us. They let us run off with no problem. My mother gave one of the guards my jewels and waited. It was a tense moment. We knew it could be a trap from the bastards to kill us all, but at the same time, it could be a reality. Maybe the only opportunity to get reunited with our father, uncle Filip, Magda, Therese and uncle Ernst. The Herscha family was almost destroyed, there were not that many of us left alive since World War I. It was not that our men liked to fight wars; they went to war because they had to go, and our rulers made them go.

Almost all the people from camp met at the departure point. It was an opportunity no one dared to let go, freedom or death. I would estimate that at least three quarters of the population that had been held captive had died of hunger, from torture or had been murdered by the Communist Serbian guards. We had seen our own people vanished or murdered one after another, for almost two years. Almost every day we would see the funeral carriage waiting in front of the infirmary. Our deceased were just thrown one over the other without any respect, followed by German-Yugoslavians with shovels. Even though we saw new people being brought from other concentration camps on a daily basis, there were not that many of us left. Until now, Kruschevlje had been the last stop for all German-Yugoslavians.

Finally we started to follow a guard, afraid of the sentinels who were ignoring our departure. My mother told me to follow her very closely and asked me to take care of Kathy. She managed to be first in line after the guard. Our clothes were not fit for any winter, much less this one. Not only was the cold unbearable, but the wind was bone chilling because we had no flesh on our bodies to protect us. We had to keep moving to stay warm.

At day break we could finally see who was walking with us. To our surprise there were more guards walking along with us then we thought. When we started our journey to Hungary, we all tried to stick together afraid of getting lost in the dark, but after we had been walking for a while, the group started to scatter into a thin line with the strongest leading the way and the weak and ill lagging behind.

My stamina was high, I wanted badly to get out of Kruschevlje, the four of us had to make it to the end, and there was no doubt in my mind about that. I looked back with curiosity to find out who else was walking with us. Following us very closely was Emmy carrying her son Herbert in her arms. Behind her were two families with a total of five children, including the two girls who were raped at the farm. The rest of the people following us had been living, if it could be called living, in other rooms throughout the camp. At that time we didn't know what happened to those who decided to stay in Kruschevlje. Were they shot dead? Did the Serbian Communist soldiers kill them before they abandoned camp? We hoped they had received some sort of help to survive that crude winter. Many years later I heard that those who had stayed behind had been moved to another concentration camp.

Eventually, my sister started complaining and refused to keep going because of the cold weather. "Come on Kathy! We have to walk, they said if you stay behind you are not going to make it and you will be lost for good...You can make it Kathy! Come on! Stop complaining and don't let go of my hand...let's follow mother. We're not far away...we have to make it! We're almost there, come on!" I was trying to reassure my sister all along our long, bitter and frostbiting walk to freedom. The whole time that she was crying and complaining, she never for a second stopped sucking her thumb. I kept on pulling her, walking and struggling with my flip flop shoes, taking pains to keep the snow out of my toes and pulling Kathy by my nearly frozen hand, without a sweater or gloves.

My mother was in front of me, carrying a rucksack on her back. Inside the rucksack she was carrying little Gertrude to protect her from the cold weather and make it easier for her. She would switch the rucksack from one shoulder to the other, or sometimes she would cradle it in her arms to alleviate her tiredness. I heard Emmy complaining, so my mother tried encouraging her "Keep on going Emmy! You are going to make it! We are almost there, don't give up now! Let's go, we are on our own! If you stay behind no one is going to help you and you may freeze to death, follow me Emmy!" but Emmy continued to say that she couldn't go any further.

I had heard in our room that Emmy was a rich classy lady. She didn't know how to do many things women do for a daily living. I lost her out of my sight but I knew she was following me. At one point, I turned back to look for Kathy and saw icicles hanging from her nose. I took them off as well as the ones hanging from my own nose. I looked for Emmy and her little boy, but neither of them were anywhere to be seen. That was the last time I saw her or her boy. I don't think I was strong enough to help her or pull her kid and my sister at the same time. My shoes were making me lose much of what was left of my strength. Our bodies did not have any muscles left. We were skin and bones walking to freedom, like phantoms covered by worn out rags without any color on them. Yes, a long line of phantoms barely walking in the ice cold winter morning.

Finally we reached the border of Hungary and got to a village called Hegyeschalom, if my recollection is right. It seemed to me that we had walked for several hours. I really had no idea of the lapse of time; all I remember is that it was more frigid than ever. It was a big relief to us when we saw people were waiting for us at the border telling us to get into a barn. The barn was cold too, but at least it blocked the wind and felt warmer than the outside weather to our nearly hypothermic bodies.

I don't know who those farmers were or who told them that we would be there, but they had everything prepared for us. I imagine they lived around there. They were so considerate to us all and gave us food. I will never forget that delicious, reviving hot soup they gave us. It seemed that we never had enough to eat, we were very hungry and all food tasted delicious to us on that arctic winter day.

At nightfall, we all went to sleep on the straw, covering our bodies with it. We were so exhausted that we woke up late the next morning, hungry again, weak from fatigue and cold, astounded to see the farmers' wives carrying big coffee pots with hot coffee and bread for all of us. They also gave us clothes to change into and dispose of our rags.

After three days of having plenty of food and being taken care of, we were on our own again with no place to go. One day a Hungarian man from the train station came and told us that we would have to wait until they could smuggle us into Austria, because none of us had a country to claim us. From one moment to the next, people started to call us stateless. We didn't have a nationality or passport or permit to be in Hungary. Austria would take us as refugees or something. The news surprised us. We just couldn't believe it.

We had to start begging again in order to survive. My sisters and I went to a house and knocked on the door asking in German, "Bitte, wir haben Hunger, könnten wir was zum Essen bekommen bitte?" (Please, we are hungry; could you give us something to eat, please?) We couldn't speak their language, nor could they understand ours, but the owners of the house must've suspected what we wanted and asked us in. We came out smiling from a joyful moment. Gertrude had a string of smoked bratwurst hanging from her neck; Kathy was carrying a pitcher of milk and I came out with a long piece of bread in my arms. We walked happily, smiling at our mother who was waiting for us outside. I remember her eyes smiling with happiness. My mother tried to give Gertrude some milk; she refused to drink it saying "I don't like white water." She didn't remember what it was any more. Later in the barn, she started to sip the milk, but only after my mother insisted that it was good for her. Kathy took her thumb out of her mouth and sipped some milk, then put her thumb back in her mouth again. Like I said, there was not enough food to satisfy our hunger. We were wasting away; eating too much caused us to go to the bathroom too often.

The day after our arrival, one of my feet felt very sore. A strong odor like rotten potatoes was coming from my toes. A farmer lady took me to a doctor; the diagnosis was frostbite. The Doctor cleaned and put some ointment on the affected area, covered my foot with a bandage and gave me socks to put on. He also gave me a used pair of black shoes so big that when I walked my feet slid back and forth inside, but I was in heaven with those shoes. A few days later, my frozen toes were fine and the smell of moldy potatoes was gone. He gave me another pair of socks and let me keep the same big black shoes.

The woman farmer who took us to the doctor was chatting with my mother, asking her to leave Kathy with her and when she settled down she could come back for her. She insisted and didn't seem to like Gertrude or me. Maybe we didn't look as cute as Kathy. My mother told her that she had gone through hell and struggled too much to survive. If she lost or gave away one of her girls, she just wouldn't be able to face my father when he came back home from wherever he was being held prisoner of war.

During the first days in Hungary, local ladies came with many outfits to give us. It was amusing to us! Hard to believe! Finally we had beautiful and decent clothes to wear. We didn't care if they were new or used, it was a moment of enjoyment and gratitude. Finally we felt human again. I was becoming an attractive girl. Right away I put on a colorful long dress. Since we were very young we didn't care to look for warm coats, but my mother did, she was always looking after us. She looked for shoes and socks that fit us well. I left my big black shoes aside while I tried on smaller shoes, in a little while the big shoes were gone.

LOWER AUSTRIA

One day while in Hungary, a Hungarian man came to the barn in a hurry telling us to get ready to leave on the next train to Lower Austria. The train was leaving in an hour. He almost dragged us to the train station. We had a lot more belongings to carry with us then at our arrival. Since we were late, the person in charge told us to get in the caboose because the train was ready to leave. He also remarked that we were not supposed to be on that train, to be quiet and not make any noise if we wanted to arrive in Austria. The same system was used until all ex-detainees from Kruschevlje were smuggled from Hungary into Lower Austria by train. My mother sat on the opposite side of us and we used our rucksacks as cushions so we could lean against the wooden side doors of the caboose.

I have no idea why Hungary had given us such a kind reception when we reached the border of their land and then smuggled us to Lower Austria, then Austria didn't make us go anywhere, instead they accommodated us in barracks. Whether Austria and Hungary had an agreement, I never found out or took the time to investigate. Austria welcomed all German-Yugoslavian descendants from different concentration camps but only to a certain extent. Austria did not help us fix our immigration papers so we could stay and get jobs as residents. We had a hard time finding jobs, and leaving Austria and going to other countries wasn't any easier. Since Germany lost the war, the Yugoslav-Partisans stole our houses. Yugoslavia didn't want us back. We lost our nationality, we had no place to go, no passport, and we didn't belong to any country in the whole world!

At our arrival in Lower Austria, we were waiting for someone to tell us to get out. When least expected a train inspector opened the door and when he discovered us inside the caboose, he exclaimed with a harsh tone in is voice:

"What are these stinky Gypsies doing in the caboose? No passengers are allowed here! Get them out! Get them out!" He then asked "Where are you going?" My mother let the other man do the talking. Finally he went away very angry, screaming and hitting the wooden wall of the caboose, making some other noises as he walked away.

After a while the train started to move again. I can't remember the name of the city where we arrived, or how many hours the trip lasted until we reached our next destination. When the train came to a complete stop, we waited listening, trying to figure out what was going on outside. Someone opened the door and told us to get out of the train. So my mother got up and reached for our rucksacks, leaning against the wooden door behind us with one hand, while grabbing the rucksacks with the other. To her surprise the door suddenly swung open and she lost her balance, almost falling out off the caboose. There was not a doubt in my mind that God was protecting us all the way, because I can't understand how come that door had never opened while we had leaned our backs against it the whole time we had ridden inside that caboose.

One thing I can't forget, and we were all surprised by, was the fact that we ended up in Frauendorf again! The same town we had not been welcome in the first time! To our amazement, people from town were waiting for us. This time all of them were very friendly and smiling. They still called us Gypsies, but gave us a house to live in and two days later they come back with food. After several days had passed, they returned again with shoes, socks, sweaters, and all kinds of clothes, including nice used dresses. To us it was a pleasant moment, as if we never had anything better in life.

My mother heard of organizations like Caritas and The Red Cross. These organizations were helping locate and reunite families who had lost contact or been abruptly separated because of the war. She started to look for our missing family through those organizations. She wanted to know if any of our relatives were alive, like uncle Filip and Magda, my father, uncle Ernst, Therese and Heinrich. She also heard that in Upper Austria ex-captives were living at the former German prisoner of war camp called Lager Haid. The prisons didn't look like prisons any more; they had been remodeled some time ago to accommodate refugees. We went there looking for our family. I never found out if the train fare to Upper Austria was paid by one of the mentioned organizations, or how my mother managed to get the train tickets for us. All I know is that we left Frauendorf and arrived in Upper Austria at the end of 1948.

At our arrival in Linz, Upper Austria, uncle Filip was waiting for us. He was living in one of the many camps close to Linz, lamenting that his daughter Grete had not made it through captivity at the concentration camp in Gakovo. To get to the camp, we had to ride in an electric streetcar and then walk about two miles to where he was living. Inside each camp there were many wooden building complexes that had been turned into barracks, each one divided to accommodate several families. He was renting two rooms, with his wife Magda and his son Walter; his in-laws, Therese and her husband Heinrich, were also living close to Filip's barracks. We were all very happy to be alive and reunited as a family. My mother wanted to keep in touch with her only family that survived the war and captivity. Unfortunately, at the barracks there were no rooms available for us because a big German community of ex-captives was living there from different concentration camps around Yugoslavia.

Soon after this happy moment, my mother found a job. Beginning a new life, she was going from being a lady of the house at Gross Betschkerek, to now working as a maid at the Mielacher estate. She was allowed to keep Gertrude in her room with her. An agreement was made with Magda and Therese to take care of Kathy. The money they would get from my mother was going to be used to buy Kathy's clothes, school supplies and anything else she needed. I would be working with the Mielacher's daughter and her husband at a house up in a hill. I can't recall their names.

On my first day of work while I was waiting in the living room to meet the owners of the house, I looked with disgust at a big painting of Adolf Hitler hanging on the wall. I thought to myself *Oh, no! Now I will have to work for him! All our suffering was his fault. How can that be!! I can't be mistaken, it is the same picture I saw at Gross Betschkerek.* I was surprised, shocked and concerned for my life knowing I would have to see him every day and serve him, wondering if my mother knew about it. I heard them coming and when I turned around I saw Herr Mielacher's son-in-law. Yes, it was him! I took a closer look at the picture and to my surprise he was not Adolf Hitler. They both just looked alike! Both had the same mustache and hairdo. Oh! I was so happy after I realized my mistake!! I worked there helping the lady of the house in the kitchen, washing dishes, doing laundry and house cleaning.

On one occasion, we were invited to a party and I had no clothes to wear, so my mother asked a lady to sew a skirt for me from one of the rucksacks. She bleached the fabric white and the skirt was nice. She also bought me an orchid blouse to combine the outfit. That was a model for other girls to wear, but I didn't like it because it was made from a rucksack from the concentration camp. I did not want anything to remind me of Kruschevlje, let alone a handy rucksack, but she asked me to use that skirt on every special occasion against my will.

It took a while for us to recover our energies, but little by little our bony bodies started to gain some muscle. I started noticing some beautiful feminine forms in my body and also recovered endurance. I never knew how much money I was earning because my mother received my salary. We thankfully enjoyed our freedom, even though we were poor. We started to work, making a decent living, and most of all, not begging for food any more to survive.

After a while Filip moved out of the Barracks and rented a house with a garage where he started a small knitting factory. With the help of Magda and two other women, they were knitting socks and sweaters. As time passed, he rented another house and hired up to thirty workers as he used to do back home. In the mean time he asked my mother if she wanted to do some work for him. He gave her plenty of socks that needed to be sewn. The socks were knitted flat by a machine, and then my mother had to sew both ends of the material together in order to make them into tube socks. Every week my mother would send the socks back and got another big bundle to work on. That helped our economic situation a little bit. We needed more money to survive.

My mother got a job at another farmer's estate called Rubenzucker. This estate was also in Upper Austria, about an hour walk from Lager Haid. She had to work in the kitchen, do some sewing, cleaning the house, looking after their five girls and several chores around the farm. I don't mean that my mother knew better but she had to cook according to the instructions of the lady of the house and there were some things she just couldn't understand, like cooking special dinners for the Rubenzuckers, and not so special meals for the rest of their workers. She and Gertrude were able to eat the same food we ate in their room, but I was not allowed to join them there.

I ate breakfast, lunch and supper with the rest of the employees. They gave us dinner plates that had already been used and chipped. Usually a meal would be a big bowl of soup placed in the center of the table. We all ate from that same bowl using soup spoons. There was a lot of slurping noises. There was a man whose sister worked in the same farm, but she had a place to cook her own food in her room. Since she cooked for her brother too, he would show up every day at our table and looked to see if he liked the food first. If it didn't look so good, he would say, "I'm going by my sister who lives across the street to eat and you all enjoy." Some of us just smiled at him.

After eating, all the employees wiped their spoons on the tablecloth and saved them to use at the next meal or they could go out to the yard where there was a trough and a faucet of running water where everybody would wash their spoons. Sometimes we would find a piece of soap beside the faucet to wash dishes, but most of the time it was missing. To avoid this inconvenience we preferred to bring our own bar of soap. The manners and hygiene of the employees was very poor. They would wash their faces and hands in the same trough before going to eat. Luckily most of them had a towel of their own. On top of that, the food didn't taste all that good. We were not used to the taste of Austrian food, we used different seasonings back home. When they gave us smoked meat it was not smoked completely. My mother had to scrub the black first with hot water. To us the meat or soup had no taste; it was boiled with no condiments at all. Our employers were not bad people, but they weren't all that good either. We had to earn our bucks. Even though we all worked very hard for more than eight hours a day, there was never a "thank you, you are a good worker." They paid us minimum wage, no matter how hard we worked. Most of the employees were refugees living in Lager Haid. They arrived on Monday and walked back on Friday, following the railroad tracks until they got home.

My job consisted of feeding the pigs at the farm, picking apples, cutting the grass using a sickle, turning the hay with a rake, making apple cider of good quality for my employers and regular for their workers. I had enough chores to keep me busy all day long and part of the night. At the end of my workday, I was worn out and just ate and slept good to be ready to start working hard the next day.

This situation made me very sad. We used to own a house, nice clothes, fine shoes, nice furnishings, pleasant living room and dining room, fur coats. Now, home was only a small room for my mother, Gertrude and me and my father was still missing, being held captive somewhere in Germany by the American Army. My only moments of happiness were those I spent on my free days from work, I used to walk on the field by myself, feeling free, loving Mother Nature, alone and with no one to disturb me.

CAMP HAID

Adam Herscha, my father, was set free from prisoner of war camp at the end of the summer of 1949. He started to look for us or any member of the Herscha family immediately through Caritas and the Red Cross. They told him that uncle Filip was living at a camp near Linz, Upper Austria. He went looking for him and uncle Filip led him to us at the Rubenzucker's estate. When we saw him, it was a moment of bewilderment! I looked at him ecstatically; I just couldn't believe what I was seeing. My mother was kissing and hugging him with love! He called me extending his arms. All of a sudden happiness bathed us. We thanked God and cried out of happiness and suffering. It was almost impossible to believe that we were reunited again after so much suffering, and most of all, that we were all alive and well! Kathy and Gertrude didn't recognize their own father any more. My mother had to introduce him to them, my father was sad. From now on, we would be together forever, I thought. At least that was our wish, what we wanted, and what we believed in. The same day my father came back, the Rubenzuckers invited us for supper; it was the first time I was allowed to be seated with them in the dining room. They seemed to want to please my father however they could.

For a while, my father lived with uncle Filip, Magda, Therese and Kathy; my mother kept working for the Ruben-zucker estate. In the autumn of 1949, my father found a job at a factory called Stahl Werke (steel factory), which hired a lot of German-Yugoslavians. The pay wasn't good and you had to work very hard, which was the reason Austrians didn't like to work there. After my father got the job, we were able to apply for a room at the barracks at Lager Haid. In a few days we all moved there, including Kathy. I didn't work any more and Kathy went to school, my sister Trude, as we called Gertrude, started kindergarten.

My father's job at Stahl Werke was one of those jobs that nobody else liked to do. As any other man in Lager Haid, he had to take any job that was available. All parents needed money to feed their families and we were not an exception. The distance from Haid to Linz was too far to walk and expensive to ride the train. As soon as he was able to, my father purchased a bicycle to ride back and forth from home to work. During the summer months it was fine to use the bicycle, but during winter he had to take the train.

Camp Haid Church

After working all day, he was so tired the only thing he wanted to do when he returned home was to take a bath. The bath situation was also a little bit of a problem since it was several minutes away in another barrack. Once there, most of the time he had to wait in line to go in. It was even worse during the winter months when he had to go outside in the cold weather right after taking a bath. My father had never had to work that hard in his life.

Camp Haid was like a village; there was a church, medical clinic, school and a soccer field. There were more than fifty barracks that surrounded the soccer field, some of them had toilets inside. There were six barracks that were called the poor section; we lived in one of those. The toilet was located about four barracks away and the bathroom was located in a big garden between the poor section and some of the other barracks. The toilets consisted of a long board with round holes, where eight people could all sit at the same time forming a row, each hole separated by a small piece of vertical wood for some privacy. Between barracks, our neighbors planted flowers and there were also benches where people sat to sunbathe. We didn't have a fancy church to pray in, but every Sunday we went to church. Our clothes were old, but very clean. It was not a big deal because all the young people dressed like that. At camp my parents found friends from back home and met some new people they became friends with. German-Yugoslavians helped each other. Sometimes they would go together to buy chips of wood to burn in the kitchen stove. They asked for a discount and shared the cost with friends. They all had to spend their money intelligently in order to make the most out of it.

At Haid, all we got was a single room to live in, but it was big enough for us. My father modified it, dividing it into several rooms, finally giving us some privacy. I was proud of my father.

He and some friends made a good deal on the wood, they paid only five schillings for it. With that wood he and his friends divided the big room that was appointed to us and made a house inside the barracks with doors, small closets and shelves to hang our clothes. They also made a table and four stools, kitchen cabinets and three top shelves, a closet and two windows for which my mother made curtains. He also bought my mother a stove and a funnel to take the smoke and odors out of the kitchen. We were living poorly, but he always managed to make our house a pleasant place to live in. My mother also tried to make our home pleasant. She always took great pains to feed us as best she could even though we could only afford to eat meat on Sundays.

THE AUSTRIANS

Austrians never missed an opportunity to make money. On the outskirts of camp there was a little house where a butcher shop would open on Friday afternoons. We could buy all different types of meats there. On the opposite side of Haid there were two more stores. There was a grocery store that was owned by Herr Penz, the only German-Yugoslavian doing business there, and a butcher shop called the Repa Store that was next to his. We could buy all sorts of meats there too, including smoked sausage. There was also a baker, Herr Furtmeyer, who drove his van around camp every day selling fresh bread, buns and the like. He came at the same time every day. After we had been at Camp Haid for about a year, a huge store opened that was like a department store. There we could get anything we wanted, food, clothes, house furniture and kitchen utensils.

At Haid, we could find almost anything we needed for every day living, but we were very short on money to buy food. That was a common problem for all families in Lager Haid. Finding a job was very difficult, if not impossible, and if you were lucky enough to get one, it didn't pay very well. Any Austrian could go and apply for a job and get it with no difficulty at all; any German-Yugoslavian requesting for the same vacancy would be denied the opportunity to work, but if the applicant was lucky enough to get the job, then he would get a salary that was about one quarter of what any young Austrian would earn for the same activity. Young Austrians preferred finding labor away from the farms, so farm jobs were somewhat more available to us, earning only one quarter of what the job was really worth. Applying for jobs at the "Arbeits Amt" (Unemployment Services) in Linz wasn't any easier. When a German-Yugoslavian would go and submit an application for a job that was posted, the first thing the clerk would ask was for identification or permit to work. None of us had passports or any form of identification. Usually the clerks would say that the job was already taken. They knew we were in exile with no documents.

Several years later, young German-Yugoslavians started to leave Austria looking for work elsewhere. We found out that the best jobs Austria had for us were not helping us improve our way of life. We knew it long before they did, but at the time we had no other choice due to our refugee status and because we did not have any legal documents to prove who we were or where we had come from. Luckily, other countries like the United States, Germany and Canada gave us the opportunity to leave the country. Austria gave us a passport for six months that we could use to go any place out of Austria that we chose. After six months, the document would expire regardless of where you were. Most of the exiled German descendants decided to move abroad, someplace in the world where there were better opportunities to be prosperous in life. From that moment on, Austria started to run out of young workers. We were the only cheap labor they could find. When this situation became an issue for the country, the government started to make things easier for us. In about 1953 the government offered citizenships to those who wanted to stay. By that time almost all exiles had moved abroad or recovered their German citizenship from Germany, but once again Germany accepted my people back there only with the condition that they had to work for the coal mines located in Oberhausen. That was what I heard about that situation, because by that time, my family and I had already immigrated to Canada.

STEFAN

At Camp Haid, there was a party every Saturday afternoon. All the youngsters gathered together in a big hall close to the barracks where we lived. My only girlfriend Marianne and I used to go there for fun, to dance and meet the boys. Some of them were from Gross Betschkerek. My girlfriend was about my age, so we got along very well. I liked her because she was very discrete and we kept each other's secrets. She was an excellent friend, unfortunately she and her family moved to Winnipeg, Canada. I was well known among the boys, some of them were good friends, and they knew how to behave toward females.

Our annual carnival party was a big deal to all of us. We dressed up in our best clothes and the party was ours. During one of those carnival parties the lights went out because of a thunderstorm, so the boys lit their cigarette lighters or struck matches to illuminate the place. The music never stopped playing. Someone took my hand and we danced until the lights came back again. Then I finally saw who I was dancing with. He was older than me, introduced himself saying, "my name is Stefan, from Vukovar, Croatia."

His hometown was about 140 kilometers from mine. I guess if there hadn't been a war, I would have never met him. I liked him from the beginning. He behaved and treated me differently from the other young boys. Stefan and the other guys made my feet hurt from dancing all night long. I loved to dance, so I was having a great time. After a while I lost track of him. Later on I found out he had a girlfriend and had been with her for quite a while. So, I thought he was not meant for me.

Therese and Stefan Schmidt

The following week Stefan was inquiring about me to the girls. They told him that if he wanted to find me, he better go where the guys were. There, he could find me in the middle among all the handsome boys. And it was true, I preferred to have male friends then the "blabbermouth" females. When I saw him I greeted him with a smile. He asked me to dance and he didn't move from my side all night long.

"I heard you have a girlfriend," I said, "what's her name?"

To my surprise he answered, "Therese."

I smiled at him and asked, "Is she coming tonight?"

"No, we broke up yesterday." I only looked into his eyes and smiled. I kept quiet hoping for him to go away, but every time the music stopped he wouldn't let go of my hand.

Shortly after that dance, one day I was walking down the street and came across his Therese. She approached me and asked me to leave Stefan alone. I asked her what the reason was that she couldn't keep him. She just looked at me and walked away without answering. That was the last time I ever saw her. Her family ended up moving out of Lager Haid. Many years later, Stefan told me, "If you wanted to meet someone at that carnival party with the lights on, you would never have found someone better than me."

OUR FAMILIES

When Aunt Therese found out Stefan and I had started dating, she invited us for Sunday dinner. It was wonderful, I was happy to have a boyfriend for the first time in my life. "Kodel" (Godmother), as we called Therese, was my mother's Godmother. She pulled me to the side and started asking me questions about his family. Before she had a chance to ask me, I told her that he had five brothers and three sisters and that he was the son of a blacksmith from Vukovar. The names of his parents were Andreas Schmidt and Rosalia Gross. She didn't like that his father used to be a blacksmith. She didn't smile or anything, she just paid attention with interest. I guess Kodel wanted to know whether he came from a rich family or how they used to live back home. I didn't know about that, and I didn't care. I realized that I was not at Gross Betschkerek any more; our lives had changed. I was just another person in the world that sometimes didn't know where to turn in my life. Unfortunately, Therese was looking for wealth, so she advised me not to marry him because his family was not a good match for our family.

Kodel always went by what you had and who you were. I remember her reminding me, "and don't ever forget that." She told me that so many times. How could I ever forget? On my side of the family, my father was the first one to oppose my relationship with Stefan. Now I understand him, as parents we never think there will be anyone good enough for our kids.

Stefan's mother was the opposite, she was very happy with me. She loved me right away. She was a wonderful mother in law.

She used to call me Terike in Hungarian. What I liked best was that she never interfered in our marriage, she also used to say to her daughter Leni, as we call Magdalena, that she admired me more than her other three daughters-in-law. Irene, one of her daughters-in-law, was also pleased with me. She was married to Andreas, Jr. her first born. Irene told me, "Stefan is going to marry into a wonderful family." She also said that Stefan had a very hard time supporting his family ever since his father died. Andreas, Jr. and Irene did not have any children and they had not helped to support the family either. When Stefan and I got married, his sister Maria and one of his brothers started to work to support the family.

CANADA

Against all odds, Stefan and I got married seven months after we met at the blackout carnival party. We rented a room in barrack 129 in Camp Haid. I got pregnant right away and we were blessed with a healthy baby boy. My husband was working at a company in Linz. At the beginning everything was fine, then one day after work Stefan came home talking very enthusiastically about immigrating to Canada. "It would be a much more promising life in Canada then what Austria could ever offer," he said. So from that moment on he started to prepare his trip abroad. I was going to stay with my parents because Stefan had signed a contract to work for a family of farmers in Canada, but one of the requirements was that he had to be single. That was the only way he could get a job in Canada. When he was ready to go abroad, he told me "we will be together before we know it. As soon as I find another job, we will be living together again." Immigrating was the only way out of Austria and that also meant we would have the opportunity to improve our lives and reach for better horizons.

Soon he left to Canada under a contract with the farmer, and my son and I moved in with my parents in their barrack-house. At the time, it seemed like a good idea to me too. After waiting for nine months, which seemed to be an eternity to me, the day for me to leave to Canada finally came. Stefan got tickets for Stefan, Jr. and me to go by ship through Caritas. The only condition was that the money they spent to help people had to be returned to them through a payment plan.

It was at that point that I realized what it all really meant. That I had to go with my son Stefan to meet with his father, which meant going away from my parents and sisters to a place I didn't know anything about. At that moment I changed my mind, I didn't want to go anymore because it meant I would be separated from my family again. I cried and decided not to go so I could stay with my family in Austria, but that meant Stefan would be alone in Canada. It was a thorny situation for me. I didn't know what to do. My father told me that I was a married woman and that now I belonged to my husband, I had to be by his side. I looked at my son and sadly agreed that my son not only needed a mother, but he also needed a father. So, I decided to stick with the original plan. My father also told me that he would submit an application to immigrate to Canada for the whole family, and we would be together again. That gave me hope and made me feel better and gave me strength to make the journey across the Atlantic. Stefan had sent me money to buy new clothes in Linz. I bought new clothes and shoes for me and for our son. He was gorgeous. I kept telling him that his father who was living in Canada had sent us money to buy all those nice clothes. Every time my sisters asked him who bought him those clothes, he would say, "my papa, who lives in Canada."

It was around 1952 that our journey to Canada began aboard a cargo ship called Arosa-kulm. I was crying from the moment I left my family all the way until I got to Quebec, Canada. The trip on the Atlantic lasted seven days, but I wasn't able to enjoy the blue waters because we were hit by a terrible storm that made me sick for most of the trip, forcing us to stay in our cabin. On the last day the storm was finally over and I felt much better. Early in the morning, we went out walking along the deck to enjoy some fresh air. Seeing the beautiful sunny sky and the blue ocean made my heart feel full of new hope as Canada was welcoming us. After we arrived and passed customs and immigration, we went looking for the railroad station to take us to the outskirts of Montreal, where Stefan was waiting for us.

By the time we boarded the train we were starving. A sandwich vendor walked past us down the aisle. I couldn't quite understand what she was saying, but on her way back I stopped her and picked a sandwich that looked appetizing through its thin wrapping. We ate it hungrily but the bread was soft and sticky so it got stuck to the roof of my mouth and was not as good as the bread in Austria. I looked at Stefan and he was chewing happily and sipping milk from a carton. I smiled and took another bite even though I didn't really like the bread. At that moment I was taken back to Kruschevlje when I was eating the tiny piece of hard corn bread that was divided among ten people. The sandwich I was eating now was a feast in comparison, so after a while I got used to it and was able to enjoy the delicious sandwich even more.

The train ride lasted around five hours. When we finally reached our destination I got off the train desperately looking for my husband. It was not long before we saw each other. We kissed and hugged glad to be together again. He introduced me to the owner of the farm, who was a quiet old man. I asked Stefan to ask our son who had bought his clothes. He talked to his son for the first time, telling him how nice his clothes were and asking him who had bought them. Our little one answered happily "my papa who lives in Canada." We all laughed and walked to board the farmer's car. Stefan took me by the hand and told me "finally we are here, there will be bad times, but never like we suffered in Austria." His words made feel safe and happy.

After we had been at the farm for about a week, Stefan told me that the farmer and his wife were inviting us to go to the village for some ice cream. When we got out of the car, he noticed the look of disapproval on my face and warned me "not to look surprised or stupid" if it wasn't what I expected, because that was how they were welcoming both of us. I looked around the village and realized I was lost in the middle of nowhere. I saw several houses scattered here and there, and a general store across from the train station. The place looked completely desolate to me, even though it only took about half an hour to get there from the farm. That village was the closest contact with civilization for who knows how many miles around. They ordered our ice cream at the general store which was the only place where you could buy ice scream, groceries, hardware, etc. We ate it standing up; there wasn't even a table or any chairs to sit and talk for a while.

Stefan's new job at the farm was not far from Montreal, where his sister and three brothers were living. It was a hard job with many responsibilities. Stefan was pretending he knew about farming, even though he had never worked as a farmer in Yugoslavia where he had been a shoemaker apprentice or in Austria where he had been a factory worker. On one occasion he was doing something and the farmer went to talk to him with a dictionary in hand, trying to explain to him that he was not doing it right. Stefan pulled out his dictionary and answered him "in Austria we do it like this."

To me the farm was beautiful! It was quiet and full of trees and nice landscapes, but the monotony of the farm life started to get on my nerves. You couldn't see a person for miles around. I was more used to the city life, surrounded by people. I was used to communicating with people, having good conversations and sharing time together with family and friends. The only enjoyment for me at the farm was being with my son all day long, playing and talking with him. The only people at the farm were the owners, who were an elderly couple, four workers and us. Every afternoon I walked around the land admiring the scenery, it was something unforgettable. Sometimes I recall those moments of quietness with contentment. I loved those moments, but not enough to spend my entire life there.

We lived in a big room in the main house. The other employees lived in the same house in the basement. The only way I could communicate with the farmer's wife was by using a true German-English dictionary I had. At first I didn't have any responsibilities around the house, but not being able to really communicate got me into working, and the worst part was that I wasn't getting paid. It all started one day when the farmer's wife showed me places around the house that I had never been in before. In the kitchen I saw the first electric freezer, it was a monster, extremely big. Everything in the freezer was packaged and marked. There were meats of all cuts, veal, chicken, pork, turkey, rabbit, duck and pigeons. The smoked meat was hung as Schinken, Wurst and anything you could think of. She asked me if I could cook. I thought she meant for my family, so I said yes. That same day she asked me to cook, to my surprise she meant for everyone in the whole house, including the field workers. That was how I started to do something useful, contributing to the household. Everyone liked my cooking; they complimented me saying that I was a good cook. I don't know if it was true or if they were just saying that because I had never cooked for eight people in my life. Maybe they were just tired of the way the farmer's wife cooked.

The owners were very nice but I was tired of farms, I had worked in farms in Austria too. I had just had it with farms. I asked Stefan to get me out of there; I just couldn't stand it anymore. When the owners found out we were going to leave, they explained their plans for Stefan and me. They told us that Stefan was going to inherit the farm; the boundaries were as far as you could see and Stefan was going to be the sole beneficiary in their will. They didn't have anybody else in the world; it was only the two of them. I felt bad, I had a feeling Stefan wanted to stay there, but he said that if I wanted to go, we would move to Montreal, where there would be better opportunities for us and a good education for our son.

The farmer lady went looking for me in our room and asked me not to leave. Since I had made up my mind, I told her that I was very happy there, but I did not like farms because they brought bad memories for me. She seemed to understand my reasons and gave me $150.00 for our travels and a good start in our new life in Montreal. That was a fortune, because $10 a week was all we needed to live on in those days. The farmer was to take us in his truck to the train station; he wished us good luck and said he was sorry we were leaving. I saw his wife on the porch, standing alone; she did not say a word, just waved her hand from far away. She was wiping tears from her eyes.

Around the time that we were moving to Montreal, Germany was accepting as citizens all soldiers who fought in their ranks during the Second World War as my father had, including their families. My father obtained that German citizenship but didn't move to Germany because he had promised me that we would be reunited, so he applied to immigrate to Canada and also submitted an application to immigrate to the United States of America. My family never heard anything from the Canadian immigration department, but after four years of waiting they were all accepted to immigrate to the United States.

MONTREAL

At our arrival in Montreal, we stayed with Stefan's family for two months. The only money we had was the last salary he had earned at the farm. As soon as Stefan started to work we rented our own apartment and arranged to pay back the money Caritas had given us to pay for the ship tickets. It took about a year for us to finish paying Caritas back, then we decided it would be a good idea to get into the habit of saving money, so we opened a bank account with the only money Stefan had which was $10.00. To his surprise, I gave him the $150.00 the farmer's wife had given me. I had been hiding it from him just in case of an emergency.

Two years later, we moved to a nicer apartment in St. Laurent, a suburb of Montreal. There I met Clare, a Jewish woman who needed somebody to clean her house three times a week. She had three little children and was a wonderful woman. Her brother-in-law owned several apartment complexes, so we moved into one of those apartments. I felt as if I was in heaven! It had a balcony surrounded with bushes and trees, a new refrigerator, oven, bathroom, new carpeting. Everything was so nice and beautiful. Since I was working for her we paid only half of the rent. We met another couple, Gustel and Eddy, living in the same complex, but later on they moved to South Carolina, U.S.A. Eddy asked my husband if we wanted to move with them to South Carolina. He told us that there was a better way of life in the United States and it was worth moving there. We decided to stay in Montreal since we had already applied for our visa to become residents of the United States because we had received news from my parents that they would soon be moving to Chicago. Another couple we met at the complex and became friends with were Irene and Georg, who now live in Vancouver, Canada. We all used to go out together and had picnics during the weekends. They were also very good company.

As soon as we heard that my family had moved to Chicago, we hoped the U.S. Department of Immigration would give us our residency as soon as possible so we could also move there. We had no idea there was a quota and a long waiting list of people ahead of us that had applied for the same purpose. As soon as the law allowed, my parents and sisters became American citizens. Shortly after that, I heard that President Johnson was going to help reunite all families who had been separated from their loved ones because of the war. This gave us the opportunity to jump out of that long waiting list and be accepted faster since the new law was for American citizens only.

I was dying to see my parents and sisters. As soon as we were able to take a vacation, we traveled by train from Montreal to Chicago to visit my family. I felt like myself again, happy to be with them. Finally we were close to each other or almost close. We spent our entire vacation together, which lasted three weeks.

When we were accepted to live in Chicago as residents, the U.S. Department of Immigration asked for a person who was going to be Stefan's sponsor so my father volunteered. As a sponsor, he would be responsible for providing food and shelter if Stefan couldn't provide those things for himself and for us. My father would also be responsible for paying any hospital bills in case he got sick or anything else that he couldn't provide for himself. Stefan was also required to register in the army and he could be drafted to serve for the United States, which he gladly would have. Thank God he never got drafted.

My father always liked to plan ahead, so he already had a job waiting for Stefan way before we even got to Chicago. Now all we had to do was wait for the approval of the immigration paperwork for Stefan. Our son and I were accepted already. Years later we moved to Chicago where my son became an American citizen. In 1968 our dreams came true when we bought our first house on North Francisco St. in Chicago. I started to work at a factory called Williams Electronic until 1996, when I retired.

MY FATHER
1911-1985

My father was born on June 18, 1911 in Karlsdorf, Banat, Yugoslavia. As I mentioned before, he had served in the Yugoslavian army. Then, due to the Second World War, he had to go fight for the German army. He did his tour as a paramedic, which did not help us at all when the bastard Partisans took us to the concentration camp for German-Yugoslavian descendents. I consider that my father was a good man; he never meant any harm to anyone.

His mother, Amalia Quiring, was born on March 10, 1882. She married my grandfather, Nikolaus, when she was 25 years old. While my grandfather was drafted to fight in World War I, she was left behind administering their farm. When Nikolaus was on his way back home at the end of World War I, he never made it home and no one ever knew if he was killed or what happened to him. Amalia had no choice but to keep running the farm alone as it was her only means of support for herself and her two sons. She had various workers who took care of cutting the wheat in her fields. While the men would cut the stalks of wheat, the women would tie them up with rope making big bundles. They would then pick up the bundles and stack them standing up forming cones.

One day there was a big storm that was approaching her fields, so Amalia rode her best horse out to where her field workers were to warn them of the storm and tell them to return to the main house. When she got there it started to rain heavily, thundering and lightning like never before; Amalia and her workers dug through the stalks of wheat so that they could find shelter and protect themselves from the storm in the small space that formed inside the big cone. A field worker that got there after they had all gone into the "shelter" did not realize that Amalia and her workers were inside. He stuck his sickle on top of the cone causing all of them to get killed when lightning struck the sickle. She died young, making her two sons orphans. Uncle Nikolaus Herscha, my father's only brother, was raised by relatives in Karlsdorf. He was living in Germany after World War II with his wife Barbara and their two sons, Nikolaus and Josef. My uncle died around 1952. Barbara and her sons immigrated to Chicago around 1957. My father was raised by other relatives who were living at the mill in Gross Betschkerek, where he met my mother and her brother Ernst.

A man who had fought in World War II mailed my father four beautiful paintings that he had painted himself, with a note attached thanking my father for saving his life. I never found out the nationality of that man. My mother gave one of those paintings to my sister Trude after my father died in 1985. A few years later, my mother sold her house and rented an apartment half a block from our home. She then gave me the rest of those paintings.

MY MOTHER
1912-2003

When my mother was a young girl, she worked for a garment factory in Gross Betschkerek. She married my father when she was twenty-one years old. After the wedding they were living with her parents. When I was born they bought the house that was later stolen from us by the Partisan party. I assume my mother had a good life in Gross Betschkerek. My parents were often presumed wealthy people. They had, with two other couples, box seats at the live theater that they would rent for the season. She always dressed according to fashion and owned plenty of fur coats, designed at her husband's factory. She always did light work in her home. She was a very strong woman and had character.

When they were living in Chicago, my mother worked at the same clothes factory as my father, on Belmont and Lincoln Avenues. My father was a clothes cutter and my mother was a quality inspector. On the first day of work she told the supervisor that she was leaving. Her supervisor thought she was taking her lunch break, but my mother never returned that day. Instead she went shopping on Lincoln Avenue. She did this several times until she was told that she had to return to work like everyone else. She never took her working responsibilities seriously.

My parents bought a two flat on Claremont and Addison, where my mother lived until 1987, two years after my father passed away. My parents were very active in the Chicago German Society; they founded the Gross Betschkerek club together with some of their country fellows, Frank Mattias, Herbstler Fritz, Jochum Peter, Meiszner Franz and Steyer Michael as well as others. When they had the first opening party in September of 1966, they invited all the other German Social Clubs in town. They were also active members of the American Aid Society of German Descendants and the Donau-Schwaben Social Club, where my mother belonged to the Donau-Schwaben singing-choir formed by German women. They were busy singing every Christmas, Mother's day, Easter and Kirchweih Fest. Every year on Memorial Day there was a picnic of the American Aid Society of German Descendants in Lake Villa, Illinois, where they held a big mass in honor of our people who died during the war and in concentration camps. On this day they had previously made wooden crosses that would represent each concentration camp in Yugoslavia. Every year my mother carried the cross that represented Kruschevlje, in memory of her mother Katharina.

During the whole time we were held in captivity, my mother had managed to hide several pictures of the family. She had been able to save a black and white 8x10 of my father and her with my two sisters and me for 54 years. She gave me some of those pictures before she passed away, she must have given away the rest of the pictures because I know that there are many missing pictures. Long ago she also gave me the pearl-clip that belonged to my grandmother Katharina, from which I had a ring made. Those are the most precious jewels and the only ones that my mother saved from all the family jewels.

I almost forgot to mention that my mother met face to face with one of the eight women that were taken away from Kruschevlje. Many decades had passed since that horrifying day at the concentration camp and they met in Chicago. She told my mother that from Kruschevlje she was taken to Siberia, Russia to work as a servant for one of the officers. The other women ran the same luck and had worked as servants or done hard labor. The Serbian Communists hadn't cared about splitting families apart or abandoning young children. Those eight women never returned to Kruschevlje.

Another thing I have to mention is that after my grandmother died in Kruschevlje, my mother was always asking about her young brother Ernst. No one was able to tell her anything about him, until my father arrived at Haid from the war. He told her not to look or wait for Ernst any more, because while he was a prisoner of war he heard that Ernst was lost in Yugoslavia on his way home. No one knew where his corpse was laying in Yugoslavian soil.

MY SON STEFAN

As I mentioned before, Stefan, my husband, proposed marriage as soon as we got to know each other. We went to parties every weekend to dance. After a short time our marriage took place in the Catholic Church at the barracks in Camp Haid, Austria. Not too long after we got married, Stefan Jr. was born. A midwife assisted me, as was common in those days. I went into labor on a Saturday at 2 a.m. and by 8:45 a.m. that same day, my son had been born. At first, he was not breathing and he was blue. The midwife spanked him on his behind. After several spanks he started to cry. I just couldn't believe when I saw him the first time. I held him in my arms, feeling his nine pounds alive and moving. I was proud of his big body, I held him thinking that he was a little doll. I started to sing to him:

"Guten abend, gute Nacht,
mit Rosen bestickt, mit Liebe
bedacht und schlafe gut heute Nacht..."

I sang kissing him many times. That was the song that came to my mind. I was so happy! He walked when he was ten months old. When he was one year old he had learned to talk, we never talked to him in "baby talk." He learned very quickly; he could bore any person that started to talk to him. My son was never an Austrian citizen, because Austria never allowed us to become citizens, for political reasons, I guess.

From the moment we arrived, Canada opened its doors wide for us by allowing us all to apply for the Canadian citizenship five years after our arrival. I found a job at a factory sewing zippers on jackets. It was not bad because with that money Stefan started to go to Kindergarten in a German school. He loved it there. I was pleased that I was also helping to support our family and that the money I was earning helped a great deal.

Stefan was an excellent student and as he grew up and became a man, he naturally fell in love with a young girl by the name of Sydney Klein. They got married in St. Benedict Catholic Church on Irving Park Road. They rented an apartment for a few months and bought their first house on the north side of Chicago. A year and two months later, their first son, Steven Christopher, was born. Four years later my second grandchild was born, Michael Scott.

RETURN TO GROSS BETSCHKEREK

As I mentioned in the beginning of this book, in 1987 we were able to return to our hometown. I went there on vacation with my husband Stefan and grandson Steven. The main purpose of this trip was for our grandson to visit our hometown, see the house that was stolen from us, and meet my husband's family in Vukovar, Croatia.

After a week from our arrival there, we encountered a couple that we had met while they were visiting relatives in Chicago; they offered to be our guides around the city of Gross Betschkerek and were very pleased to see us. They told us that they would take us to our old neighborhood. I was kind of uncertain about the location of the streets and where to go, but I managed to spot the house of our neighbors, the ones that displayed the Hungarian flag opposing the welcome party for our soldiers on the day the German Army took over the city. Since they also knew our ex-neighbors, they knocked on the door and when an elderly lady opened the door, I saw her sister was following behind her. Excited our guide asked her:

"Do you know who this young lady is?"

The two ladies looked at us puzzled, raising their eyebrows as if trying to solve a mystery. The lady who had opened the door exclaimed:

"You are Terike!"

She remembered my name in Hungarian. She smiled and opened her arms to hug me. "How are Adam and Maria? We always wondered if they are alive. We never heard about the family after you left the city."

They welcome us into the house and the introductions took place. They invited us for coffee and cake. Over the conversation they asked me if I had a picture of the family. I showed them a picture of my parents' 50th wedding anniversary. They looked carefully at both of my parents, my sisters and I with our husbands, the grandchildren and two great-grandsons. My mother gave me that picture in case I found someone who wanted to see it or for me to show it around. At my return home, my mother was upset because I gave the two sisters the picture to keep.

We went on a tour of their house and when we were in the back yard I looked at the fence that separated our houses, but to my surprise a high wall was erected instead that blocked my view to the old manual water pump in our backyard. I asked them who was living in our house, they answered that a couple but that they were not at home, and they didn't know what time they would be back. From the street I looked at the house and noticed that it was in bad shape, the grass on the sidewalk was about two feet high, with weeds and grass covering the stone street.

We drove to my maternal grandparents house on Lemandorf. It had been a corner house, but it was demolished and instead a beautiful bungalow was constructed there. I walked to the cemetery wall to take a look, remembering that the Serbians had thrown my grandfather over that wall and into the cemetery. I felt very sad, my eyes became watery as I remembered all our suffering of the past, and I said a prayer for my grandfather.

Our impression out of this trip was that the "poor Partisan members" to whom our properties were given by the Communist Partisans cared less to keep them in good shape. The houses and the farms were not properly taken care off. Since they had to give half of the harvest to the government, they got smart and moved the fences further in from the roads to make the working land smaller.

If you compare the houses or farms that people owned before the war with those to whom the properties were given by the Serbian Party, immediately you would see a big difference in the quality of harvests or maintenance of the houses. Now Yugoslavia was far behind on agriculture compared to when the Serbians stole them from hard working German-Yugoslavian people. In Vukovar we could observe that businesses that were privately owned were open for business early in the morning. Instead, those owned by the government and managed by civilians were not opened until after ten or eleven in the morning.

It was a nice vacation after all. The most important thing we did was to show our grandson where we came from.

EPILOG

Bad memories haunted me for decades after we walked to our freedom. On the few nights when I could actually sleep, I was tormented by constant nightmares. Other nights I suffered from insomnia and had flashbacks during the long nights when I laid awake. I tried to get it into my head that it was all over, trying to forget that there had been a war and that I had endured everything that happened during those horrendous days of my young life. I tried to convince myself that there wasn't anything I could have done. I, like my fellow German-Yugoslavians, could only do as I was told and had no choice but to suffer the consequences of the war which was now over.

There was nothing normal about my childhood during those years in Kruschevlje. I was not playing with dolls or playing with other children my age. I was confined to the house because being outdoors was too dangerous and even if it hadn't been, I didn't have the strength to think about anything except how hungry I was. I was a child who was barely surviving, suffering as a result of the lost war against all German descendants of Yugoslavia. I barely had anything to shield my body from the glacial cold of winter and was always afraid of being killed by the mad Partisan soldiers while being held captive.

For some time I was resentful against Germany, but in my blood runs the same blood of my long time ancestors. My customs, ideology and way of life are German. From the moment Yugoslavia was invaded by German soldiers, German-Yugoslavians became part of Germany. Yet, at the end of the war, Germany did not claim us as its fellow citizens and instead treated us as outcasts! Our men, including my father, were drafted into the Army to fight in the war, and then at the end of the war were exiled and left without any knowledge of their families. Without a country or a nation that wanted to take them or their families as citizens, but as the years passed I changed my way of thinking. I am German, I feel German, I love Germany, and I love Gross Betschkerek with the same intensity as I love Canada and the United States of America, where we were received with open arms and offered citizenship. I love them for giving us the opportunity to work our way out as honorable fellow citizens of Canada.

I kept this part of my tormented life to myself, as a secret for me alone for many years. For decades I dealt with the hidden shame and the terrifying recollections of my younger years, frightened of being threatened by the Partisans if I ever talked. Thinking that no one could understand the effects that the war had caused in me. Scared to tell anyone, not even my understanding family, let alone the rest of the world, until now. Now I feel as though a big weight has been lifted off my shoulders, sharing my misery with twelve members of my family and the rest of the world.

I consider myself a lucky woman surrounded by all of my loved ones. In our blood runs German Blood and in our minds German ideology as always.

970134

Made in the USA